# DOES YOUR BUSINESS SHOW UP OR **STAND OUT**?

Simplifier, Satisfied, and Aspiring™ is a pending trademark of circle S studio

Lansing Building Products® is a registered trademark of Lansing Building Products, LLC

Hourigan® is a registered trademark of Hourigan Group, Inc.

Slack® is a registered trademark of Salesforce, Inc.

Yammer® is a registered trademark of Yammer, Inc.

Net Promoter® is a registered trademark of Nice Systems, Inc.

Google® and Google Analytics® are registered trademarks of Google, Inc.

Kodak® is a registered trademark of the Eastman Kodak Company

Sony® is a registered trademark of the Sony Group Corporation

Canon® is a registered trademark of Canon Kabushiki Kaisha

Blockbuster® is a registered trademark of Blockbuster, LLC

Netflix® is a registered trademark of Netflix, Inc.

ChatGPT® is a registered trademark of OpenAI OpCo, LLC

OpenAI® is a registered trademark of Open Artificial Intelligence, Inc.

Intel® is a registered trademark of Intel Corporation

Agency Management Institute® is a registered trademark of Agency Management Institute, Inc.

Disney® is a registered trademark of Disney Enterprises, Inc.

Atlantic Bay Mortgage Group® is a registered trademark of Atlantic Bay Mortgage Group, LLC

Roc Solid Foundation® is a registered trademark of ROC Solid Foundation

Coca-Cola® is a registered trademark of The Coca-Cola Company

Prius®, Lexus®, and Toyota® are registered trademarks of Toyota Jidosha Kabushiki Kaisha

Apple®, Macintosh®, iPod®, and iPhone® are registered trademarks of Apple, Inc.

Gore® and Gore-Tex® are registered trademarks of W. L. Gore & Associates, Inc.

Easy Button™ is a trademark of Staples, Inc.

Hardback ISBN-13: 978-1-966168-05-8

Paperback ISBN-13: 978-1-966168-04-1

Library of Congress Control Number: 2024926221

INDIE BOOKS INTERNATIONAL®, INC. 2511 WOODLANDS WAY, OCEANSIDE, CA 92054

www.indiebooksintl.com

*Dedication*

## TYLER & MICHAEL

*Thanks for the greatest gift of all—to be your mother.*
*You remind me daily of the potential that lies within*
*and to always better my best.*

## MICHELLE

*You've taught me the meaning of a true business partnership.*

## TAMI, KATIE & RACHEL

*May our circle of respect be unbroken.*

# Contents

# The Secrets Of Stand Out Companies

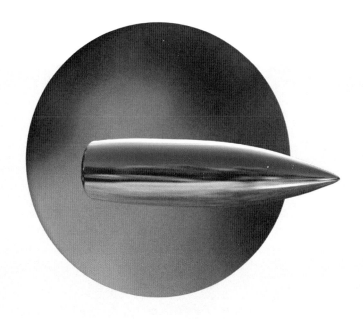

"There are no shortcuts to success."

—*Annika Sörenstam*

Wouldn't it be amazing if we all had a magic formula for business growth? While it's a wonderful thought and something we would all like access to, it just doesn't exist. There are no shortcuts and no silver bullet. It's all about doing the little things well with a big dose of discipline. That's certainly what has been observed over my forty-year career as a business owner and consultant, and why I agree with the old saying, *the harder you work, the luckier you become.*

Over the years, I've had the privilege of working with thousands of leaders and hundreds of companies, and once thought growth was all about leadership. While that's a piece of the puzzle, it's not the whole picture. Driven by a burning curiosity and the incredible strategic partnership of my colleague, Tami Berry, we began gathering insights from our consulting work and existing third-party research to better understand the "little things" that certain companies seemed to get right all the time.[1]

---

1. Mary Ann Anderson, Dr. Edward Anderson, and Dr. Geoffrey Parker, *Operations Management* (Hoboken, NJ: Wiley, 2013).

STAND OUT FACT

We're surrounded by businesses every day—we work for them, visit them, and some own them. Of the more than *thirty-three million* that exist in the US, *25 percent* last more than *fifteen years,* while only *1 percent* reach *$10 million* in revenue.[2]

What emerged was a list of nine traits that, on the surface, seemed simple. But the companies that were showing up as a "best place to work" or taking top honors in their industry were doing all of these at an exemplary level. It reminded us of what it's like to live a healthy and long life. While as leaders we all know the basics, very few of us do them consistently well. Every day.

---

2. "Frequently Asked Questions About Small Business, 2023," U.S. Small Business Administration Office of Advocacy, March 7, 2023, https://advocacy.sba.gov/2023/03/07/frequently-asked-questions-about-small-business-2023/.

There are many data points and case studies surrounding our research, but in a world overflowing with information and lengthy explanations, this book is not about that. It's a playbook, written the way I like to consume information—give me just enough to gain context, then get straight to the point, and let me decide where to go next.

Each chapter is written and designed to give you scannable information that is easy to consume on what high-performing companies consistently do. In "The What" section, each trait is described the way we have observed it in our consulting and branding practice. The "So What" section gives real-world examples of how each trait has driven success, in some cases for our own clients or for companies that we have long admired for standing out. The "Now What" section provides recommendations on books, resources, and tools that we have found useful and will hopefully guide your journey as you think about taking each trait to a best-in-class level. Each chapter concludes with a section to take notes as you reflect on how your own company exhibits each trait and how to do it better.

The goal is to respect the time of busy leaders by providing concise, actionable insights that keep you engaged and bettering your best.

*Enjoy the journey!*

## Book Format

# The What

An introduction to the trait based on our own research and third-party information.

# So What

Why the trait matters as shown through real world examples and stories of how it has led to continued improvement and growth.

# Now What

Practical recommendations, books, resources, and tools for creating a best-in-class experience for everyone.

# INTRODUCTION

## The Heart
## Hooks The Mind

W ith over three decades of advising business-to-business (B2B) firms, our strategic approach has focused on guiding the experiences a company creates at every touchpoint—because they all matter. By capturing the intangibles and creating an emotional connection with clients and prospects, you open up minds that ultimately open up more doors for future growth.

In addition to guiding experiences, our consulting practice monitors the nine most common traits that are found among the highest performing companies worldwide, based on our own research, as well as other third-party sources. When done consistently, these companies not only outperform their peers, in many cases they become designated as best-in-class.

## Nine Traits Of High-Performing Firms

① Define clear guiding principles.

② Optimize the employee experience.

③ Exceed client expectations.

④ Embrace change.

⑤ View the ecosystem holistically.

⑥ Track a data-rich dashboard.

⑦ Collaborate on quality.

⑧ Cut through the noise.

⑨ Learn and improve continuously.

While we have seen these nine traits remain tried and true, regardless of the economic cycle or latest fads, we know that historically, massive disruption can alter the landscape. It can also spur some of the greatest innovation, which can lead to a shift in our long-held beliefs.

The global pandemic is a perfect example of how profoundly the world can change. Every day brought up new conversations around work. What does the employee experience look like now? Where should work take place (home, in-office, or hybrid)? How do we lead across multiple communities? And how do we maintain and

The global pandemic brought a new word to the workplace for everyone: *Purpose.* Employees are seeking a higher level of purpose in their work. Unfortunately, only *18 percent* of companies are providing it at a meaningful level. Recent studies show that *62 percent* are seeking more purpose and that's where firms that have defined a clear purpose around the "why" will have an advantage in today's war for talent.[3]

---

3. Naina Dhingra, Andrew Samo, Bill Schaninger, and Matt Schrimper. "Help your employees find purpose—or watch them leave," McKinsey, April 5, 2021, https://www.mckinsey.com/capabilities/people-and-organizational-performance/our-insights/help-your-employees-find-purpose-or-watch-them-leave.

measure processes and productivity in the now "new normal"?

As worker attrition rates rose to record highs of 33 percent during the pandemic, research showed the main cause for leaving a job, or even the workplace in general, was related to employees desiring a more purposeful experience that aligned with their personal values.[4] To understand how this disruption was impacting business leaders' views on what it takes to be a high-performing company today, we partnered with a third-party research firm to survey top B2B executives around two core concepts:

1. Were the tried-and-true traits of high-performing companies still important following the massive disruption that took place in the workplace following the pandemic?

2. How do leaders define the notion of being best-in-class as it relates to standing out in the marketplace, attracting and retaining top talent, and providing top-notch products and services to their client base?

## The Research

The results of our research show there are three distinct attitudes toward the concept of being best-in-class and the traits considered most important for a high-performing company. We identify these segments as

---

4. U.S. Bureau of Labor Statistics. *Monthly Labor Review*. June 2022. https://www.bls.gov/opub/mlr/2022/article/job-openings-and-quits-reach-record-highs-in-2021.htm.

Satisfied, Simplifiers, and Aspiring, and they were almost evenly represented across survey respondents, with no statistically significant variation attributable to gender, age, years of experience, or size of their organization.

The data shows that 72 percent of respondents, regardless of segment, believe that a best-in-class reputation matters, yet if it's stated as a marketing claim, they're skeptical.[5] When backed up with credentials, it can help attract and retain the people and partners your business needs to grow.

Armed with this information and the nine traits of high-performing companies, our consulting team zeroed in on helping clients create higher levels of the brand, employee, and client experiences, *by design*. Focusing on these three experiences led to a noticeable shift in our brand work. While still crafting unique identities through logos, colors, and pixel-perfect website designs, we found the ability to truly differentiate them in the marketplace was directly correlated to finding better ways to express their guiding principles of purpose, vision, mission, and core values.

While these elements were already in place at most firms, they lacked what I would call *true* meaning. It was interesting to see the difference in companies that seemed to be "checking the box" on the guiding principles exercise as being "one of those marketing things" versus those that took it very seriously. The

---

5. circle S studio. Best-In-Class Research. 2023.

clarity of language created momentum, much like the flywheel effect described by Jim Collins in *Good to Great.*[6] And in most cases started to put these clients ahead of the competition.

## A Better Experience = Higher Growth

As our research revealed, each type of leader places a different emphasis on where they should focus their efforts in pursuit of high performance:

*Satisfied leaders* believe a reputation for being best-in-class is demonstrated by a track record of strong revenue performance as an indicator of customer satisfaction. Sustained financial performance and high-visibility leadership are as much a part of their brand identity as core values. The employee experience is a secondary focus.

*Simplifiers* are laser-focused on a few key initiatives to hone their internal processes. The brand and employee experiences are secondary considerations.

*Aspiring leaders* place a high value on the brand, employee, and client experience. They believe the guiding principles are foundational and serve as the North Star for where the company is and where it's going. In their minds the best companies continuously adapt and innovate to remain at the top.

---

6. Jim Collins, *Good to Great: Why Some Companies Make the Leap And Others Don't* (Harper Business, 2001), 164-187.

## Satisfied: **35 percent**

**Satisfied professionals are the most likely to say their organization is already one of the best in their industry.**

They feel most companies focus on a well-defined employee experience to the degree they should, and say clients expect organizations like theirs to be driven by core values. These respondents are least likely to feel employee development should be an ongoing process and that the best companies adapt more quickly to marketplace changes and opportunities than other organizations do.

*"Best-in-class means you have strong leadership at the top and are excellent at driving continuous profits year-over-year. There's also technology that is best-in-class and diversified lines of business."*

To see where your company stands on each of the Nine Traits, you can take the quiz by scanning the QR code. For an on-line version, visit https://circlesstudio.com/best-in-class/traits-of-high-performing-companies-quiz/.

## Simplifiers: **33 percent**

**Simplifiers dismiss the importance of a best-in-class designation, saying it has neither meaning nor value.**

They feel the best organizations achieve success by having a simple, proven process for serving their customers and by focusing on a few key initiatives at a time. These respondents believe that for most companies, the mission statement is not a top consideration when making decisions and that a brand is simply considered in a marketing context.

*"The term best-in-class isn't based on anything. It's a marketing claim, and no one can define what it means."*

## Aspiring: **32 percent**

**Aspiring professionals value designations such as best-in-class and consider them meaningful.**

They are strongly aligned with the nine traits as indicators of being best-in-class. In general, these respondents also believe that most companies don't focus on employee experience and satisfaction as much as they should.

*"An organization that is best-in-class means happy employees and customers driven by a healthy company culture that is lived out every day."*

The world underwent a profound change in the latter half of the 20th century, as we shifted from the Industrial Age to the Information Age. Our manufacturing-based economy was replaced with information technology where data and knowledge workers reigned supreme. Yet, as the 21st century matured, an intriguing shift began to take place. We had an abundance of data, perhaps too much data, and the Experience Age emerged. No longer was it sufficient to simply have access to all of the information, now, things moved to how that information was encountered, interpreted, and actually integrated into our daily lives. This change was propelled by advancements in virtual reality, augmented reality, and a cultural pivot toward valuing experiences over possessions. The digital world started to blend seamlessly with the physical, making every interaction rich, personalized, and deeply immersive. The Experience Age was not just about consuming content, but about living it, and the global pandemic accelerated the importance of a purpose-driven workplace.

# The Age Of Experience

All three mindsets have contributed to growth for high-performing companies throughout the efficiency-focused Industrial Age and into the technology and data-focused Information Age. However, in today's Experience Age, we believe those with an Aspiring mindset have an advantage. The ability to attract and retain quality talent has been identified as a top challenge for all businesses and in today's world, it's never been more important.

To overcome this obstacle, the experience is no longer optional and must be both meaningful and measurable at every level of the journey. Those that are delivering the best experiences are winning the talent war and building loyal customer and client relationships for the short- and long-term. They're not just *showing up*, they're *STANDING OUT*.

# PART 1:

## Set The Foundation

# 1

## BUILD YOUR BRAND
## ON GUIDING PRINCIPLES

# PURPOSE
# DRIVES
# MOMENTUM

> "Purpose-driven organizations bound by values
> are stronger than profit-driven organizations
> bound by rules."
>
> —*Alexander den Heijer, international speaker,*
> *author and consultant*

We've learned over the years that most people associate the brand of a company with the name, logo, and the visual elements that get attached. But it's much more than that. A brand is also the overall perception that others have of your company that's shaped by every interaction and touchpoint. Stated another way, your brand is the emotional and psychological relationship that your business has with *all* stakeholders, built over time through consistent and meaningful experiences.

Whether it's through exceptional customer service, intuitive digital platforms, or high-quality products and services, prioritizing the experience fosters loyalty and positive word of mouth. And in a crowded marketplace, businesses that consistently offer better experiences create lasting impressions, build stronger relationships, and ultimately gain a competitive edge.

Sounds pretty straightforward, right? Well, not so much. The tricky part is understanding what *every* interaction looks like. In marketing, it's called Journey Mapping, which is the process of documenting and analyzing the various touchpoints and interactions an employee and customer has with a company throughout their entire relationship.

The way we see it, a better experience begins with a strong brand experience (BX) that lays the foundation for a better employee experience (EX), and those two experiences create the proper momentum for a better client experience (CX). These expressions of experience feed and build on each other, creating momentum for your business when done exceptionally well.

## BX (Brand Experience)

n. the totality of all sensations, feelings, thoughts, and actions evoked by a brand.

Beyond the logo, visual identity, and messaging, the brand experience includes every interaction and touchpoint that a customer has with a company. When done well, it will shape the overall perception and emotion that customers have with a company, driving word-of-mouth referrals, long-term relationships, and ultimately the bottom line.

# The What

When you consider that many companies begin without a business plan, a strategic plan, or a set of guiding principles, it's not surprising that 45 percent fail within five years. It reminds me of the famous passage from *Alice in Wonderland* when Alice is faced with a fork in the road, and she encounters the Cheshire Cat with this query:

"Would you tell me please, which way I ought to go from here?"

"That depends a good deal on where you want to get to," said the Cat.

"I don't much care where … ," said Alice.

"Then it doesn't matter which way you go," said the Cat.

"So long as I get somewhere," Alice added as an explanation. "Oh, you're sure to do that," said the Cat, "if only you walk long enough."[7]

The Cheshire Cat is right, surely you'll get somewhere, business owners and leaders, but probably nowhere near the destination you had in mind. The way I see it, if you want to stand out for the long term, your brand must have clearly defined guiding principles—meaning your purpose, vision, mission and core values are not only written down but they are known by everyone in the organization. You're not just talking it, you're walking it. They are the framework for how your organization operates, how decisions are made, and what behaviors are non-negotiable for your associates and all key stakeholders of the company.

Thinking you've already done this exercise and are ready to skip ahead to the next chapter? You may want to think again. If your guiding principles were created many years ago, it might be a good time to revisit and reflect on what you have and determine if the language is still resonating, especially in today's ever-changing world. Several years ago, a client shared with us their mission statement that was written decades ago. One thing to note, this company is a global industry leader with an enviable record of success, but the document

---

7. Lewis Carroll, *Alice's Adventures in Wonderland* (London: Macmillan, 1865), 48.

was filled with a lot of "we must do this" and "we must do that" wording. We called it the "musty" mission—it was outdated language, and they agreed it was time for a refresh. If your language is misaligned with contemporary values and norms, you will likely stand out, but for the wrong reasons.

Having a positive experience at every interaction with your company is critical when it comes to winning and retaining clients. According to research, 86 percent of people will leave a brand they were once loyal to if they have two or three bad experiences.[8] It's called "ghosting"—they walk away without explaining a single word. In a split second they ask others who they would recommend and then they do a quick Google search to check out the competition. You were in one day and suddenly out the next. It's that fast.

There are four primary guiding principles that govern modern business today: purpose, mission, vision, and values. Each one builds on the other, and together, they make a powerful foundation for momentum that will set you apart from the competition with better experiences, by design.

---

8. "Experience is everything. Get it right." PwC, accessed September 9, 2024, https://www.pwc.com/us/en/services/consulting/library/consumer-intelligence-series/future-of-customer-experience.html#:~:text=In%20the%20U.S.%2C%20even%20when,after%20just%20one%20bad%20experience.

## *Guiding Principles*

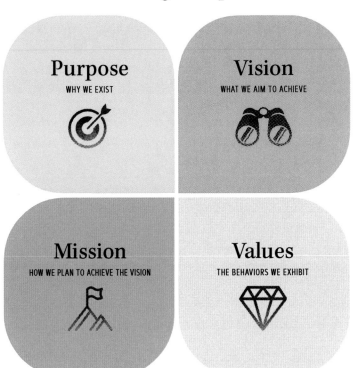

Some leaders may struggle to distinguish between the different principles—particularly in how they strategically target different aspects of managing their organizations. When each principle is expressed clearly to all levels of your organization, they can help attract and retain employees, as well as clients. Because you've defined who you are and where you're going as a company.

## Purpose

The purpose is the "why." Why your organization exists. What lights a fire in your belly and gets people motivated to be a part of your company? Simon Sinek says it best when he notes that, "People don't buy what you do; they buy why you do it. And what you do simply proves what you believe."

Your organization's purpose should largely explain the reason that you're in business, the problem you want to solve, and how you choose to engage within your industry and with the broader world.

Being able to articulate your why—the inherent purpose of your business—will not only attract more valuable talent to work for your company, but will make it easier to achieve your mission. For this reason, purpose should be at the center of everything you do.

## Vision

Your vision should clearly define the "what." What are you aiming to accomplish with your vision? What is your ultimate goal? Your vision can and should change over time, and should be a part of the three-year, five-year, or ten-year plan for your business. It will provide the North Star that guides your journey and encapsulates your company's trajectory in a way that's easy to articulate to your team.

## Mission

Your mission gets into the "how." A lot of times, this is where companies begin: How are you going to show up in the market? How will you ultimately achieve the vision? You want to be able to create something that's truly authentic. More importantly, you want to build a culture intensely focused on the manner in which you do your best work.

Many businesses use words to explain their mission—ultimately landing on worn-out (or as we call it, "bankrupt") language that simply states the table stakes, the minimum it takes to compete in their industries. Your mission should clearly state the differentiating factors, processes, or experiences you bring to the table to set yourself apart in the broader market.

## Core Values

Your core values are the non-negotiables of your business. They are how your purpose, vision, and most importantly, your mission are lived out at all levels of your company. The core values you choose should define the behaviors that show up in the day-to-day—not the every-now-and-then.

These values clearly and succinctly articulate who you want to attract in the broader market. If an individual or organization does not share your core values, they probably aren't the right match for you.

## The Interplay Between Purpose, Vision, Mission, And Core Values

When you can identify and articulate the why, the what, the how, and the who of your business, you catapult yourself ahead of your competitors and become better positioned for growth. Collectively, when your entire organization can identify and live these principles, you gain extreme power in the market.

By ensuring clarity on all four guiding principles, you create the greatest opportunity in your business to propel long-lasting, sustained growth. Clarity of vision—from onboarding to the day-to-day operations of your organization—is key to achieving success.

In our work as a consulting and branding agency, we see time and time again that the companies who live and breathe guiding principles are the ones outperforming the competition. They are the "Aspiring" mindset that showed up in our research. We see these companies consistently rank as a great place to work. They cultivate outspoken promoters of their brands both internally in their teams and externally in their clients, vendors, and partners.

Consistency and clarity in your organization's voice leads to everyone on your team singing from the same song sheet—it creates a power and amplification that research has proven leads to higher metrics across all aspects of the business.

# Where Does Your Organization Stand?

We routinely ask three questions to leaders of companies interested in assessing where they stand on their organization's guiding principles.

First, can everyone in your company recite any of your guiding principles off the top of their head? Second, is your language truly and uniquely differentiating in a way that expresses what you do differently from the competition? Third, if these guiding principles exist in your company, where do they exist and to what degree?

Finding the answers to these questions can be difficult, and will involve careful research into how your brand permeates each level of your business.

By understanding where your organization stands on your guiding principles—by keeping the pulse on how these factors drive your brand, employee, and client experiences—you can orient your organization to face adversity head-on and propel growth in the long-term, no matter the state of your industry or the broader market.

# So What

Most companies acknowledge having different elements of guiding principles, but it's often a check-the-box exercise done at the start versus a true compass for the organization.

I remember asking one of our long-standing clients, who had grown from a small local firm to a recognized mid-Atlantic leader, about their guiding principles, and they agreed it was time to revisit things. They came back saying, "Great news, we took our ten core values down to seven." When I asked them to name the seven, they could only come up with a few. I said, "You just did this exercise as a management team and if you can't remember them, how do you expect anyone else to?"

I'm not going to tell you a definitive number of core values that your company should have, but I do have an affinity for the number three. Determine what's right for your organization and make the values memorable— so that your employees (who are always on the front lines)—clearly understand how to embody them when interacting with clients, vendors, prospects, and the public at large. Because we all know words matter, but actions speak louder.

## *Here's how we embrace guiding principles at circle S studio.*

**Our purpose** is to passionately deliver exceptional experiences that propel growth and create cultures that inspire.

**Our vision** is to be the best-in-class experience agency serving companies that are always striving to get to their next level of success.

**Our mission** is to better our best everyday by constantly learning and asking what's next and why.

**Our core values**

Respect: *We earn it by giving it to everyone.*

Collaboration: *Together we're stronger— an unstoppable force.*

Drive: *An innate fire in the belly means we're always seeking to raise the bar.*

If you're reading this book, chances are your company is still in business. That's good news. The tough news is how hard it is to survive for a long period of time. Here are the stats on business longevity:[9]

- 23.2 percent fail within the first year
- 45 percent fail within the first five years
- 65.3 percent fail within the first ten years
- Only 25 percent make it beyond fifteen years[10]

Now let's look at closely-held family businesses:[11]

- 30 percent of family businesses survive the transition from first to second generation ownership.
- 12 percent survive the transition from second to third generation.

With those stats in mind, you'll enjoy the following case study for this amazing business even more.

9: Devon Delfino, "Percentage of Businesses That Fail—and How to Boost Chances of Success," LendingTree, updated April 8, 2024, https://www.lendingtree.com/business/small/failure-rate/.

10: Michael Deane, "Top 6 Reasons New Businesses Fail," Investopedia, June 1, 2024, https://www.investopedia.com/financial-edge/1010/top-6-reasons-new-businesses-fail.aspx.

11: Jack Nicholaisen, "The Family-Owned Business - Analysis of Their Success and Longevity," Business Initiative, updated June 25, 2024, https://www.businessinitiative.org/statistics/demographics/family-owned/.

# Lansing Building Products

Meet Lansing Building Products, a family-led company supplying exterior building products to professional contractors. Founded in 1955 by Ted Lansing, the company has grown significantly over the decades, expanding its reach across the United States. Today, Lansing operates 114 locations in thirty-five states, providing a comprehensive range of products including siding, windows, roofing, gutters, and more.

Our introduction to the company began when third-generation Hunter Lansing was taking over as CEO from his dad. We were brought in to help with a refresh of their brand and we began, as always, with internal research to determine what their authentic DNA was all about.

The company prides itself on its mission of delivering superior service while maintaining the highest ethical standards. This commitment is driven by core values of respect, service, and excellence, and for the first time in my career, we were working with a company where *EVERY* member of their team could recite their core mission statement. But we were also struck by the fact that the words existed, but did they really exist in the company? Here's how Hunter Lansing remembers it:

*"I'll never forget, we were sitting in my dad's conference room and circle S had a slide deck to present their research findings. At that point in time, our corporate offices were in the same building as our Richmond, Virginia, branch where we distributed products. We had been there since my Grandpa Ted, our founder, bought it in the early '70s, and it had some age on it. There was a railing going up to our showroom that had gotten rusty over the years and was a little crooked, but it's one of those situations where if you've been in one place for forty years, the eye starts to not notice these things. I'm not embellishing this story at all, the question was asked, "Do we understand that excellence is one of your three core values?" And we said, yes. Then we saw the picture of the rusty railing and they said, "Is this what excellence looks like to you?"*

*We wanted to crawl into a hole, but said, "You're exactly right. Absolutely, 100 percent that is not what excellence looks like."*

Photo: Tami Berry.

**37**

Well, Hunter and his dad didn't kick us out, and we had many excellent discussions from there on how, even in the little things, it's so important to align your values with everything you do.

The Lansing management team seized the opportunity to make sure their guiding principles had a clear purpose and that everyone was on "the same page." What emerged next was an internal process to identify behaviors that aligned with their mission of respect, service, and excellence and *True Blue* was introduced throughout the company. Today there is a common language that everyone has embraced and understands what it means to live the values of the company.

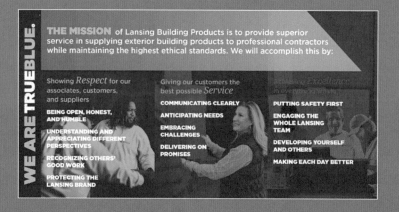

Following a brand refresh and management's concentrated efforts to bring their guiding principles to life with a common language known as "True Blue," Lansing Building Products achieved *300+ percent* organic and external growth, over an eight-year period.[12]

## Are These Immutable Laws?

We believe your purpose and core values should not change. And the thing is, whether you have them written down or not, they are there, floating around in your company culture. When you identify and narrow them down, it's easier to remain laser-focused. That's when there's real power to shape your company for the better, so that you **STAND OUT** rather than merely show up.

---

12. Interview: Hunter Lansing, interview by Henry DeVries, August 3, 2023.

# Now What

Ready to go deeper? Here are more resources to help you evaluate your current guiding principles and consider how to elevate them continuously.

## Recommended Reading

- ***Start with Why: How Great Leaders Inspire Everyone to Take Action*** by Simon Sinek (Penguin Group/Portfolio, 2009). Through his writings and TED Talks, Sinek has brought the importance of defining a company's purpose to the mainstream. In this book, he explores why some leaders and organizations are able to inspire more loyalty, innovation, and success than others. Sinek argues that, rather than the typical focus on the what or how, these companies and individuals start by explaining the why. This clear sense of purpose inspires both employees and customers.

- ***Built to Last: Successful Habits of Visionary Companies*** by Jim Collins and Jerry I. Porras (Harper Business, 1994). Based on a six-year research project, this influential book identifies companies' common habits and practices that have thrived over decades. Collins and Porras define key characteristics that set visionary companies apart, focusing on long-term strategies that can build sustainable success, even through difficult periods of change.

- ***Good to Great: Why Some Companies Make the Leap… and Others Don't*** by Jim Collins (Harper Business, 2001). Collins explores why some companies are able to go beyond being good to becoming great. Based on extensive research, he identifies foundational principles such as leadership, disciplined people and thinking as contributors to long-term greatness.

- ***Traction: Get a Grip on Your Business*** by Gino Wickman (BenBella Books, 2012). The Entrepreneurial Operating System (EOS) is a set of simple, practical tools business leaders can use to manage and grow their companies more effectively. Wickman focuses on six key components—vision, people, data, issues, process, and traction—to help organizations overcome common challenges and achieve sustainable growth.

If you need some inspiration to refresh your company's guiding principles, visit the websites of companies you admire to see how they communicate theirs. As you review, consider how the company demonstrates each element (purpose, vision, mission, and values) in its culture.

**Build Your Brand On Guiding Principles**

**2**

ELEVATE THE EMPLOYEE EXPERIENCE

# YOUR COMPANY'S
# HEARTBEAT

> "When people are financially invested, they want a return. When people are emotionally invested, they want to contribute."
>
> —*Simon Sinek*

We all know the adage that "Happy employees make happy customers," and in this chapter, we delve into why companies should take this mantra to heart and what it means to deliver an outstanding employee experience.

**Spoiler alert:** It's more than delivering a comprehensive employee manual during your onboarding session that details your benefits package and how to navigate the company's technology system. It's about every single iterative part of the experience—from recruitment to retirement.

By focusing on every aspect of the employee experience, companies can cultivate an environment where employees are satisfied, motivated, and deeply committed to the success of the organization. This

## EX (Employee Experience)

EX is defined as an employee's perception of the company experience throughout their tenure. This encompasses everything from recruitment to onboarding; day-to-day work, including career training and development; to ultimately off boarding, regardless of how or why the employee exits the company. Some of the most critical elements that define a strong EX involve the physical work space, company culture, as well as tools and resources that increase productivity, morale and overall engagement. When created and managed with intention, EX communicates to current and prospective employees how they are valued by the firm.

commitment translates into higher productivity, lower turnover rates, and ultimately, a more successful and sustainable business. As we explore the various facets of the employee experience, you'll discover practical strategies and insights to help your company thrive by prioritizing the well-being and engagement of your most valuable asset—your people.

**STAND OUT** FACT

Organizations with high employee engagement are 21 percent more profitable and grow profits up to three times faster than their competitors. Additionally, high engagement levels reduce absenteeism and turnover, further contributing to financial success.[13] According to one study, the average cost of replacing an employee can range from 16 percent to 213 percent of the employee's annual salary, depending on the position and industry.[14] Bottom line, if you invest in them, they will invest in you.

# The What

When you study companies that are consistently recognized as a "best place to work," you'll find very little is left to chance. Beyond clear guiding principles that live at every level of the organization, they also keep a pulse on employee satisfaction. Using real-time data they strategically create new programs and initiatives that will enhance the company culture and overall employee engagement. Here are some of the most common characteristics that exist in each of these high performing EX companies.

---

13. Matt Tenney, "How Employee Engagement Affects Profitability," Business Leadership Today, accessed August 23, 2024, https://businessleadershiptoday. com/how-employee-engagement-affects-profitability/.
14. Heather Boushey, and Sarah Jane Glynn, "There Are Significant Business Costs to Replacing Employees," American Progress, November 16, 2012, https://www. americanprogress.org/article/there-are-significant-business-costs-to-replacing-employees/.

### ① Strong Leadership And Management

The whole concept of leadership is what inspired us to dig deeper into why some of our clients (and companies that we know and admire) were consistently showing up while others were truly standing out. As stated in the beginning of this playbook, leadership is not all of it, but it's a powerful part of the equation. We know that strong and supportive leadership inspire a positive work environment. In fact, it inspires all of us. Think about a favorite teacher or coach that got more out of you than anyone thought possible. What were they doing differently?

In the book *Multipliers: How the Best Leaders Make Everyone Smarter* (2017), co-authors Liz Wiseman and Greg McKeown describe a concept called the "multiplier effect" where leaders, who are Multipliers, focus on the energy and genius of others, while Diminishers believe their genius is rare and what's needed the most to keep operations moving forward and growing. You can probably think of who these leaders are in your organization right now.

While it may seem counterintuitive, when you relinquish control and empower others to learn and grow without you being in the middle of everything, the organization will thrive and see faster growth. The companies that are investing heavily in leadership training to create more "multipliers" are going to have a competitive advantage because their teams will excel in skills like communications, strategic thinking, emotional intelligence and how to effectively mentor and guide others for a greater good.

### 2 Comprehensive Benefits Packages

If you want to attract and retain the best talent, you have to offer a competitive salary and benefits package, but it's more than that. The best way to view all aspects of the full compensation package is in relationship to what the marketplace is delivering for your industry and geographic location. The hybrid workplace today can complicate how you view things, so the best bet is to work with consulting firms that conduct industry and geographic-specific compensation reviews. Additionally, find ways to enhance the health and wellness side, as mental health support, wellness programs, and gym memberships are contributing significantly to employee well-being and job satisfaction.

### 3 Collaborative And Innovative Work Environment

High performing companies place a priority on the physical workspace. When you consider the number of aging buildings with poor ventilation, mold, and lack of natural light, it makes sense that we have a lot of unhealthy workers. The science and research have proven that open office designs create better communications, because they break down the "us vs them" siloed approach to business. We also know that green spaces with natural light promote better thinking and a sense of belonging that keeps workers engaged and connected. And this is just the beginning of what makes a better space and outcome for all.

### 4 Flexible Work Arrangements

How we approach the workday fundamentally changed when the global pandemic took all of us by storm. Today, we can no longer request that every member of the team show up in person to work eight hours a day, five days a week. You may want that as a company owner or leader, but you're going to have a hard time finding that team. The genie is out of the bottle and there's no going back.

The new norm is how to incorporate flex time into the work week that's a combination of remote, hybrid, and in-person. Yes, every company is different and if you're in the construction industry it's hard to build a ten-story headquarters remotely, but the point is this, you must build flexibility and adaptability into the human side of the equation, your people.

The work force isn't stagnant and neither should your approach to how you work. So what's right for your firm? Bring everyone (or those that make sense to do so) together to define your process. Then step back each year and revisit where you are. What does productivity look like for all work arrangements? How are you measuring it? Ask what needs to change based on the marketplace and generational preferences—because they do matter. If all is good, keep going; if your attrition rates or productivity trends are suffering, then refine. When this is done year after year, you'll find success for your people and your firm. Guaranteed.

### 5 Employee Well-Being Programs

When it comes to enhancing the employee experience, a health and wellness program might be viewed by some firms as a nice to have, but the data shows a different story.  In research conducted by Harvard Business Review, the ROI can be as high as six to one, when there's a comprehensive, well-run program in place. Bottom line, there are many tangible benefits. Healthier employees have fewer sick days that directly reduce health care costs, translating in savings for employers. The money invested in resources such as on-site gyms, fitness classes, and health screenings, create deep bonds. Positive, supportive work cultures increase productivity and engagement, and significantly reduce attrition rates.

And services like counseling, stress management workshops, and mental health days, serve the mental health needs of your most valuable resource—your employees. Good health will show up in many places and it won't take long for your company to stand out for your genuine care and concern.[15]

---

15. Leonard L. Berry, Ann M. Mirabito, and William B. Baun, "What's the Hard Return on Employee Wellness Programs?" *Harvard Business Review*, December, 2010, 2-9.

**⑥ Career Development And Learning Opportunities**

Investing in employee growth through comprehensive training and development programs is a "must" in today's work environment. There's a great quote often attributed to Henry Ford that says it all: "What if we train them and they leave? What if we don't and they stay?"

Whether you have a dedicated "university" within the company or a continuing education budget that each employee can use to advance both their hard and soft skills, you will reap the benefits of this investment immediately.

Mentorships and coaching programs are also highly valued by employees. When personalized guidance is provided to help define career paths the employees feel valued and motivated to achieve their highest potential. It's a win-win for everyone.

# So What

## Benesch's Commitment to Employee Development Drives Engagement and Retention

As the war for talent intensifies across industries, forward-thinking organizations recognize the critical importance of delivering robust leadership and development programs. And I haven't seen many companies do training any better than Benesch, a top Engineering News-Record firm whose expertise spans a wide range of sectors, including transportation, infrastructure, environmental, water resources, and municipal projects.

When Kevin Fitzpatrick became president and CEO of Benesch in 2020, he embarked on a journey to revamp its approach to employee development and training.[16] While Benesch had always offered training, the company saw a need to "reinvigorate the program and provide more opportunities for employee development."[17] Benesch decided to take a more strategic and comprehensive approach, and they engaged a research partner to gather

16. "Kevin Fitzpatrick, PE," Benesch, accessed October 15, 2024, https://www.benesch.com/leadership/kevin-fitzpatrick/.
17. Susan Quinn, "How an Investment in Leadership Training Can Grow Careers and the Bottom Line with Kevin Fitzpatrick." Better Experiences by Design. [Podcast], April 18, 2024. https://circlesstudio.com/blog/how-an-investment-in-leadership-training-can-grow-careers-podcast/.

Kevin Fitzpatrick welcomes more than 300 managers to Energize—an in-house leadership program—which brings together managers from every department across the company for two days of immersive training and development. Photo: Benesch.

feedback from employees through anonymous interviews and surveys to better understand how they could create a best-in-class program.

The feedback from this research was eye-opening for Benesch's leadership team. Employees expressed a strong desire for more training, mentoring, and professional development opportunities. They wanted to hear from internal and external experts. They wanted access to training beyond the "hostage" lunch and learn programs, that took away from their personal time.

Armed with this valuable insight and recognizing that a one-size-fits-all approach to learning doesn't work well, they created a full-time Director of Learning and Development, which was a significant investment for a company of its size at the time. Benesch also increased training budgets and made it clear to managers that they should prioritize employee development, even if it meant reduced billable hours.

Today they have a comprehensive in-house learning and development platform known as Benesch University. Every new hire is enrolled from day one providing access to a variety of on-demand training, live sessions, and professional development programs designed to support employees at every stage of their careers. Here's a look at how the program is structured:

### ① **Grow Exec**

A year-long program for upper-level managers and future leaders, featuring a curriculum developed in partnership with prestigious business schools like Duke and Indiana University.

### ② **Grow Level Two**

A six-month program for technical and project managers, focused on developing leadership skills.

### ③ **Grow Level One**

A program for employees with five-plus years of experience, covering topics like time management, innovation, and leading people.

### ④ **Level Up**

A company-wide program offering access to thousands of training videos and courses to help employees enhance technical and soft skills, including mental health and work-life balance.

The impact of Benesch's renewed focus on employee development has been significant and the firm has seen a reduction in employee turnover, with its current rate hovering around 7-8 percent, well below the industry average.[18] Employees have also expressed greater satisfaction and engagement, as evidenced by the firm's regular employee surveys.

Benesch's commitment to employee development has also had a positive impact on the firm's ability to attract and retain top talent. During the recruitment process, prospective employees are increasingly interested in learning about the firm's training and development opportunities, and are cited often as a key factor in their decision-making.[19]

The success of Benesch's employee experience initiatives has not gone unnoticed. The firm's dedication to developing its workforce has earned it a reputation as an employer of choice, helping to differentiate it from competitors in the highly competitive engineering and professional services industry.

18. Quinn, "Investment in Leadership," [Podcast].
19. Quinn, "Investment in Leadership," [Podcast].

## Passionately Shaping Tomorrow, Today

When you invest in your people, they will likely return the favor and invest right back into the company with their energy and dedication. That's certainly Mark Hourigan's story, founder and CEO of Hourigan, who today is recognized as one of the Mid-Atlantic's top construction firms, according to Engineering News-Record.[20] And when you consider where they started, it makes their growth journey even more amazing.

With a team of five people, the company's first project was to build an entertainment and shopping center in the sandy soils on the Outer Banks of North Carolina—at a place called TimBuck 2—that was named after the two developers. As the story goes, wild horses would show up near the job site daily—and Mark Hourigan wondered if it was an omen that the business was in for a wild ride.

---

20. "Hourigan Wins ENR MidAtlantic's 2021 Contractor of the Year," ENR Mid Atlantic, June 17, 2021, https://www.enr.com/blogs/11-mid-atlantic-monitor/post/51936-hourigan-wins-enr-midatlantics-2021-contractor-of-the-year.

But the horses ended up being a very different sign, as Hourigan grew beyond anyone's wildest dreams.

It didn't take long for their reputation of building uniquely remarkable buildings and relationships started to spread, which was Mark's mission from day one for the company. And that mission has extended into the employee experience in several ways, including custom leadership development and employee well-being programs, and innovative workspaces.

## Collaborative And Innovative Workspaces

As the company grew, Hourigan reached capacity at its headquarters office space and began to assess its options. Recognizing the importance of cultural fit and the changing needs of the workforce in a competitive hiring environment, the firm made a bold decision to invest in an innovative "Office of the Future" concept for all of its locations.

Each office features a variety of spaces for both individual and collaborative work as well as intentionally created zones where colleagues can connect socially.

Top photo: Chris Cunningham Photography.
Bottom photo: Bill Dickinson, Sky Noir Photography.

Hourigan's guiding principles can be found throughout their offices and job-sites, using large graphics that highlight their core values, case studies of inspirational projects, and conference room names that tell their powerful story.

Using sustainable materials like Cross-Laminated Timber and an abundance of open spaces, Hourigan has taken health and wellness and productivity to new levels for the company.

Top photo: Bill Dickinson, Sky Noir Photography.
Bottom photo: Chris Cunningham Photography.

## THRIVE

Imagine a company culture where employees are thriving in all aspects of life. Sound impossible? Well, when the odds seem impossible, that's when Hourigan says, "bring it on." Faced with the reality that construction is one of the most dangerous industries for worker health, they envisioned creating a program that would enhance physical health, resiliency, financial health, and community for all members of their team.

The THRIVE program is a prime example of how Hourigan lives their guiding principles every day: serve with integrity, lead forward, and never disappoint. Each year they organize company sponsored events and programs around the four pillars of their program that educate employees on wellness topics such as ways to manage stress on the job site and beyond, tips for strengthening your financial health, as well as a variety of team building activities and fitness challenges. They also encourage ways to give back to the community, which is an important part of the Hourigan culture. By offering a variety of programs, employees can tailor the experience to best meet their needs.

Ultimately, the THRIVE program reflects Hourigan's dedication to its employees' health and well-being, ensuring they have the resources and support to achieve their personal and professional goals. By creating an environment that prioritizes wellness, Hourigan reinforces the idea that strong companies are built on strong, healthy teams.[21]

# Now What

Before you can figure out how to enhance the employee experience at your firm, you have to understand what currently exists. Here are several methods companies can use to evaluate how employees perceive their roles, the company culture, and their overall satisfaction:

### ① One-on-One Meetings

Regular check-ins and performance reviews with managers provide personalized feedback and identify areas of improvement for individual employees.

---

21. Katherine Gould, "Why Hourigan Wants Our Employees to THRIVE," Hourigan, August 6, 2019, https://www.hourigan.group/blog/why-employee-wellness-is-important-at-hourigan/.

### ❷ Employee Net Promoter Score (eNPS)

The eNPS is a quick way to gauge overall employee satisfaction and loyalty by measuring the likelihood of employees recommending the company as a good place to work.

### ❸ Employee Surveys

- **Pulse Surveys:** Short, frequent surveys track employee sentiment on various topics in real-time.

- **Annual Engagement Surveys:** These comprehensive surveys are conducted annually to gauge employee engagement and satisfaction.

- **Onboarding And Exit Surveys:** Surveys of new hires and departing employees help understand their experiences and gather feedback on what can be improved at the beginning and end of an employee's journey.

### ❹ Focus Groups

Conducting focus group discussions with employees from different departments can provide qualitative insights into their experiences and attitudes about the workplace.

### ❺ Internal Social Media And Communication Platforms

Monitoring internal communication platforms like Slack or Yammer can provide insights into employee sentiment and identify recurring issues or themes, including process bottlenecks or opportunities to improve communication.

### 6 HR Metrics And Analytics

Analyzing HR data, such as turnover rates, absenteeism rates, and promotion rates, can provide quantitative indicators of employee satisfaction and engagement.

### 7 Employee Journey Mapping

Detailed maps of the employee journey from recruitment to exit can help identify critical touch points and areas for improvement.

### 8 Stay Interviews

Conducting interviews with current employees helps to understand why they stay with the company and what aspects of the employee experience are most important to them.

### 9 Observational Methods

Observing workplace interactions and behaviors can provide contextual insights into the employee experience.

## Recommended Reading

- ***Built for People: Transform Your Employee Experience Using Product Management Principles*** by Jessica Zwaan (Kogan Page, 2023). Applying product management principles, Zwaan details improving employee experiences by iterating based on feedback. For leaders focused on operational excellence, this book offers practical strategies for fostering employee-centric cultures.

- ***Irresistible: The Seven Secrets of the World's Most Enduring, Employee-Focused Organizations*** by Josh Bersin (Ideapress Publishing, 2022). Bersin highlights seven strategies used by enduring, employee-focused organizations to show how they prioritize people and profits to be more resilient and innovative.

- ***Experience, Inc.: Why Companies That Uncover Purpose, Create Connection, and Celebrate Their People Will Triumph*** by Jill Popelka (Wiley, 2022). Popelka explains how purpose, connection, and celebration are key to employee engagement and company success. She uses real-life examples to show how purpose-driven companies outperform competitors by prioritizing human connection and aligning employees with the mission and values.

- ***I Love It Here: How Great Leaders Create Organizations Their People Never Want to Leave*** by Clint Pulver (Page Two, 2021). Based on his "Undercover Millennial" research, Pulver explores what makes employees stay in organizations and provides actionable strategies for leaders to create workplaces where employees feel appreciated and loyal long term.

## Podcast

- ***WorkLife with Adam Grant:*** Wharton professor Adam Grant's podcast is one of the top-rated regarding workplace culture and employee experiences. He interviews a diverse range of leaders and experts, exploring what makes work meaningful, how to improve employee engagement, and how organizations can build stronger cultures.

**Elevate The Employee Experience**

# 3

## PERFECT THE CLIENT EXPERIENCE

# AN IMPORTANT SEAT AT THE TABLE

"The key is to set realistic customer expectations, and then not just meet them, but exceed them—preferably in unexpected and helpful ways."

—*Richard Branson, founder of Virgin Group*

## A Deep Dive Into Understanding Your Client

The "client experience" began gaining significant attention in the late 20th and early 21st centuries as businesses recognized the impact of customer satisfaction on brand loyalty and profitability.

Several factors contributed to this shift in perspective. First, the competitive landscape was changing dramatically, as markets were becoming more and more saturated. Technology advancements, specifically those related to digital tools and of course the internet in general, provided companies with an abundance of data about their customers, prompting new ways to target messaging and interactions. Social media also gave customers a platform to express their thoughts and opinions. Companies were no longer the only ones deciding what communications they wanted to send to the marketplace, customers now had a seat at the table. Companies were now managing their brand equity in a different way, as a negative review could go viral in a nanosecond with irreputable damage to the brand.

Now, exceptional client experiences mattered more than ever as a key way to standing out. In our consulting practice, we started to see research predicting that by 2020 the client experience would overtake product/service and price as a reason for selecting a company and maintaining brand loyalty. And with the help of a global pandemic, that prediction became true.[22]

# The What

Research and insights from studies by organizations like Forrester and McKinsey have demonstrated the tangible benefits of investing in the customer experience, linking it directly to increased sales, customer loyalty, and an overall competitive advantage, including outperforming competitors by *85 percent* in sales growth and *25 percent* in gross margin.[23]

In order to deliver the best client experience, it's important to understand how clients perceive how well you're doing the job. When you collect the data on what they're thinking, you can tailor experiences that meet and exceed their expectations, you can personalize interactions, streamline processes, and anticipate their needs. Failure to do so often leads to what is called "ghosting," where clients simply move on to your competitors without warning. This concept is increasingly common in today's competitive marketplace, particularly from younger generations like Gen Z, who tend to abandon brands silently after just a few negative interactions. PwC reports that "In the U.S., even when

22. The CEO View of CX: What Customer Experience Professionals Must Do To Be Relevant To the C-Suite," Walker, 2016. https://walkerinfo.com/docs/WALKER-CEO-View-CX.pdf.

23. Brad Brown, Kumar Kanagasabai, Prashant Pant, and Gonçalo Serpa Pinto, "Capturing Value from Your Customer Data," *McKinsey & Company*, March 2017, https://www.mckinsey.com/capabilities/quantumblack/our-insights/capturing-value-from-your-customer-data.

people love a company or product, *59 percent* will walk away after several bad experiences, *17 percent* after just one bad experience."[24]

## Are Your Clients Promoters Or Detractors?

If you want to understand how your clients feel about you, just ask. That's where the Net Promoter Score (NPS) comes in. And it revolves around one simple yet revealing question: "How likely are you to recommend this company to a friend or colleague?" You might think, really? Can one question give real insights? The answer is, yes it can. Because when you're not hanging out with your clients, they're talking with others, and if your relationship is over-the-top positive, they will shout it to the world. They will be a raving fan for you. If there are a lot of holes to fill in the relationship, they will let others know that, too.

Developed by Bain and Company, NPS has become the gold standard in customer experience metrics for a reason.[25] Think of it as your company's report card— offering a straightforward way to gauge your client relationships and benchmark your standing in the industry.

Collecting NPS data can be as simple or as detailed as you need it to be. For many professional services firms,

---

24. "Experience is everything. Get it right," *PwC*, accessed October 15, 2024, https://www.pwc.com/us/en/services/consulting/library/consumer-intelligence-series/future-of-customer-experience.html.
25. Adam Bunker, "What is NPS? The ultimate guide to boosting your Net Promoter Score," *Qualtrics*, accessed October 15, 2024, https://www.qualtrics.com/experience-management/customer/net-promoter-score/.

this might mean sending out surveys at key points in the client relationship or even conducting one-on-one interviews. Some companies opt to use third-party consultants to manage this process, ensuring that the feedback is objective and candid. These external experts can often uncover insights that might not be immediately apparent to those inside the company.

Once you have the data, calculating your NPS is straightforward. You categorize respondents into three groups:

- *Promoters* (9-10 rating)
- *Passives* (7-8 rating)
- *Detractors* (0-6 rating)

Your NPS is the percentage of Promoters minus the percentage of Detractors, resulting in a score that can range from -100 to 100. This gives you a clear picture of your customer satisfaction and loyalty at a specific moment in time.[26]

But what does your NPS really mean? It's more than just a number; it's a window into your clients' minds. It tells you how happy your clients are right now, but the real value comes when you dig into the details. How does your score compare to others in your industry? Are you seeing improvements over time? What's driving any changes in your score?

Hearing what customers think about you can often sting. But these insights are where you should focus your efforts. Don't try to fix everything at once, just prioritize

---

26. Bunker, "What is NPS?", Qualtrics.

It's human nature—people are much more likely to share negative experiences than positive ones. In fact, according to a study by the American Express Global Customer Service Barometer, consumers tell an average of sixteen people about a bad experience but only share a good experience with nine people. Clearly, the impact of a company's customer service quality on its reputation, and bottom line, can't be overstated.[27]

---

27. "Survey: Twice as many people tell others about bad service than good," Retail Customer Experience, August 7, 2011, https://www.retailcustomerexperience.com/articles/survey-twice-as-many-people-tell-others-about-bad-service-than-good/.

one area and work on it over time. As you continue to measure your NPS, you'll see the impact of your efforts in real-time. That's how you build a stronger, more customer-focused business. That's how you STAND OUT.

# So What

If you're in business, you understand, at least in theory, the importance of delivering quality service to your clients. From where I sit, it can't be overstated enough— and from everything I've read and learned about Jeff Bezos, Amazon's founder and executive chairman, my guess is he would agree with that statement.

The reason for bringing up Bezos is because we often use Amazon as a case study when working with clients on refining or defining their purpose, vision, mission, and core values. Because when you do this well and actually live your guiding principles and not just write them down—you can literally write your own success story.

Imagine being Jeff Bezos, working out of a garage in Bellevue, Washington, with only a handful of employees and creating this vision for your new company: *to be Earth's most customer-centric company, where customers can find and discover anything they might want to buy online, and endeavors to offer its customers the lowest possible prices.*[28]

---

28. "Customer Obsession and Commitment to Innovation Push Amazon.com to #1 in Customer Service According to National Retail Survey Released Today," Amazon.com, Inc, November 02, 2006, https://press.aboutamazon.com/2006/11/customer-obsession-and-commitment-to-innovation-push-amazon-com-to-1-in-customer-service-according-to-national-retail-survey-released-today.

Wow! I still marvel at those simple yet powerful words. It's hard to imagine a time when we didn't have everything at our fingertips, but remember this was 1994, the internet was still in its infancy, and e-commerce was a novel concept. Yet Bezos saw an opportunity to leverage the power of the internet to revolutionize the way people shop. His initial plan was to build an online bookstore, but he envisioned Amazon evolving into a platform that could sell everything to everyone.

Today, Amazon is a trillion-dollar e-commerce company with a global presence, offering everything from groceries to digital streaming to AI-powered devices. Yet despite its massive growth, the core of Bezos's vision remains intact: a relentless focus on customer satisfaction and a willingness to innovate and disrupt industries. They always "start with the customer experience and work backward,"[29] and this philosophy visually lives as an empty chair that sits at the conference room table to represent the customer.

Whether you admire Amazon or not, it's undeniable that the company has fundamentally transformed retail and set new standards for convenience with a *client-first approach.*

Here's a question you want to make sure your management team is crystal clear about. *What are you trying to achieve as a business and what experience do you want your clients to have?*

---

29. Amazon Press Center. "Customer Obsession and Commitment."

# Now What

Monitoring your client experience and continuously seeking opportunities to raise the bar are essential. Here are some recommended strategies to consider: As you think about ways to elevate your client experience, it's important to start by understanding its current state. Consider these strategies for measuring where you are and identifying opportunities for improvement.

## 1 Customer Surveys And Feedback Tools

Collect feedback regularly through tools like customer satisfaction surveys, Customer Effort Scores, and Net Promoter Scores for quantitative customer satisfaction and loyalty data.

## 2 Social Listening And Sentiment Analysis

Use social media monitoring tools to track brand mentions, analyze public sentiment, and gather insights from customer conversations online.

## 3 Customer Support Data

Analyze data from customer support interactions, including common issues, response times, and resolution rates, to identify areas for service improvement.

## 4 Behavioral Analytics

Track how clients interact with your website or app using tools like Google Analytics for insights into the customer journey. Pay close attention to patterns in user behavior, such as navigation paths and drop-off points.

### ⑤ Journey Mapping

Document every aspect of customer interactions with your company, both physical and digital. This will help identify the critical touchpoints and potential pain points that shape their experience and perceptions.

### ⑥ Customer Relationship Management (CRM) Systems

Mine your CRM system for information on interactions, preferences, and history to enable personalized communication and targeted marketing.

### ⑦ Focus Groups And Interviews

Conduct qualitative research through small groups or one-on-one interviews to dig deeper into customer perceptions and expectations. These methods also provide further context to survey data.

### ⑧ Predictive Analytics

Utilize past data to create models for anticipating customer actions and preferences. Imagine being able to provide tailored experiences and resolve issues proactively.

## Client/Customer Experience (CX)

CX covers every client interaction with your business, from initial awareness and discovery through post-purchase support and loyalty. This includes marketing communications, website usability, product or service quality, customer service, and follow-up interactions. Each contributes to the overall perception of the brand and impacts satisfaction, loyalty, advocacy, revenue, and market share.

## User Experience (UX)

UX is the overall experience clients have when interacting with a company's products or services. It includes every aspect—from the usability and design of digital interfaces to the ease of navigation and satisfaction with the product or service. A positive UX can lead to higher customer satisfaction, increased loyalty, and better conversion rates. It reflects a company's commitment to meeting client needs and providing value, ultimately influencing brand perception and market competitiveness.

## Additional Resources

Here are some essential resources for leaders seeking to elevate their firm's client experience:

**Books**

- ***Outside In: The Power of Putting Customers at the Center of Your Business*** by Harley Manning and Kerry Bodine (New Harvest, 2012). This book is a CX classic, illustrating how aligning strategy and operations with customer needs leads to increased loyalty, growth, and competitive advantage.

- ***The Customer Centricity Playbook: Implement a Winning Strategy Driven by Customer Lifetime Value*** by Peter Fader and Sarah Toms (Wharton School Press, 2018). The authors discuss how focusing on high-value customers and understanding their behaviors can drive profitability.

- ***Unreasonable Hospitality: The Remarkable Power of Giving People More Than They Expect*** by Will Guidara (Optimum Press, 2022). A legend in the world of hospitality, Guidara's experience in the hospitality industry shines through this book detailing how going above and beyond in customer service creates lasting experiences, deeper connections, and brand loyalty.

## Podcasts

- *CX Cast* by Forrester: In-depth insights into CX strategies, trends, and research from Forrester analysts.

- *Outside In* by Charles Trevail: Business leaders across industries talk about the importance of customer centricity.

- *The Modern Customer Podcast* by Blake Morgan: Cutting-edge customer service strategies that can help businesses create seamless, innovative client experiences and stay informed about current trends and the latest technologies.

**Perfect The Client Experience**

# PART 2:
## Monitor The Landscape

# 4

## EMBRACE CHANGE

# KEEP AN EAGLE EYE ON THE HORIZON

"The greatest danger in times of turbulence is not the turbulence— it's acting with yesterday's logic."

—*Peter Drucker*

# The What

The pursuit of best-in-class status is a perpetual challenge, especially when you consider that the goalpost is constantly shifting. The adage "the only constant in business is change" rings truer than ever, with technological advancements, consumer preferences, and global competition evolving at breakneck speed. To stay ahead of the curve, businesses must be proactive in anticipating and adapting to these changes. Disciplined strategic planning and vigilant monitoring of the business landscape are essential for companies to stay nimble and responsive to emerging trends and sudden shifts, allowing them to pivot their strategy with precision.

Since the 1960s, a SWOT analysis (Strengths, Weaknesses, Opportunities, Threats) has been a universal strategic business tool.[30] While many find the S, W, and O easier to evaluate, today the T has never been more important to understand. In our consulting practice we think it includes not only threats, but also changing trends that can impact business.

I'll admit that I'm addicted to the whole strategic planning process. I love considering complex variables, contemplating the impact "our" decisions can have, and in general how to think several steps ahead of the competition.

You would think every company would embrace strategy at the highest level, but that's not the case. While strategic planning is widely acknowledged as essential for business success, a recent study found that less than half of businesses (45 percent) are strategic in their planning, which means they systematically analyze their environments, set goals, and develop actionable plans to achieve these goals.[31]

And while a majority of executives (90 percent) believe in the importance of strategic planning, 48 percent report spending less than one day each month focused on it, indicating a significant disconnect between the recognition of strategic planning's importance and its actual practice in ongoing business operations.[32] Which begs the question—*WHY?*

30. Dac Teoli, Terrence Sanvictores and Jason An, "SWOT Analysis," National Library of Medicine National Center for Biotechnology Information, Updated September 4, 2023, https://www.ncbi.nlm.nih.gov/books/NBK537302/.

31. Renée Dye and Olivier Sibony, "How to improve strategic planning," *McKinsey Quarterly*, August 1, 2007, https://www.mckinsey.com/capabilities/strategy-and-corporate-finance/our-insights/how-to-improve-strategic-planning.

32. Paola Cecchi-Dimeglio, "3 Ways Leaders Drive Success through Strategic Planning," Forbes, December 11, 2023. https://www.forbes.com/sites/paolacecchi-dimeglio/2023/12/11/3-ways-leaders-drive-success-through-strategic-planning/.

Here are four of the top reasons why companies fall short in the strategic planning process:

### 1 Short-Term Focus And Lack Of Immediate Value

They prioritize short-term gains over long-term planning due to pressure from shareholders or the need for immediate results. This focus on quick wins and quarterly earnings often makes strategic planning seem less urgent, because it doesn't provide instant, tangible outcomes.

### 2 Resource Constraints

Strategic planning requires time, expertise, and resources that smaller companies or those with limited budgets may lack. As a result, they often focus on immediate operational challenges rather than investing in deep, long-term strategic thinking.

### 3 Complexity, Uncertainty, And Skill Gaps

The increasing complexity and uncertainty of the business environment make strategic planning challenging. Companies may struggle to predict future trends or lack the necessary skills to conduct effective planning, leading to reluctance in committing to strategies that could become obsolete quickly.

### 4 Cultural Resistance And Complacency

In some organizations, a resistance to change and a lack of strategic thinking at the leadership level hinder deep strategic planning. Additionally, companies that have enjoyed past success may become complacent, relying on outdated strategies and seeing little urgency to adapt to the evolving business landscape.

As a business consultant, I've seen all of these factors show up in one way or another in many companies. But perhaps the one I remember most was when we were working with a firm that had merged with several medical groups, and they were seeking to rename and rebrand their operations. The branding part of the process went fairly well—but when we started down the path to drive awareness and engagement, we approached it like we always do, through a strategic lens. The CEO literally told our team in a meeting, if we say the "S" word again, it will be the last time that we meet. And it wasn't long after that we all parted ways.

## So What

In the original research that we conducted about the nine traits of high-performing companies, the "Satisfied" mindset was one-third of the respondents, which is another way to say they are basically happy where they are and doing exactly what they've always done. They are aware that they have a reputation for being "best-in-class" because of a track record of strong revenue performance and usually there is high visibility of leadership in the community and in the industry.

This mindset is the one that runs the greatest risk of being disrupted, and history provides us with many examples of what happens when a company doesn't continue to evolve.

## Kodak: A Cautionary Tale Of Missed Opportunity

Founded in 1888, Kodak dominated the photography industry for nearly a century, becoming synonymous with film and cameras.[33] In the 1970s, Kodak even developed the first digital camera, a groundbreaking innovation that could have paved the way for a new era in photography.[34] However, despite this technological leadership, Kodak hesitated to embrace the digital revolution.

Their reluctance stemmed from its deep investment in film, which was highly profitable. The company's leadership feared that moving into digital would cannibalize its film business, so they downplayed and delayed the development and marketing of digital cameras. Meanwhile, competitors like Sony and Canon seized the opportunity, aggressively pushing digital technology to consumers.[35]

As digital photography grew rapidly in the early 2000s, Kodak's market share plummeted. By the time the company fully embraced digital, it was too late to regain its lost ground. In 2012, Kodak filed for bankruptcy, marking the end of its dominance in the photography industry.[36]

---

33. "From the Camera Obscura to the Revolutionary Kodak," Eastman Museum, accessed October 15, 2024, https://www.eastman.org/camera-obscura-revolutionary-kodak.

34. James Estrin, "Kodak's First Digital Moment," *The New York Times*, August 12, 2015, https://archive.nytimes.com/lens.blogs.nytimes.com/2015/08/12/kodaks-first-digital-moment/.

35. Carsten Krause, "Case Study: Kodak's Downfall—A Lesson in Failed Digital Transformation and Missed Opportunities," *The CDO Times*, September 27, 2023, https://cdotimes.com/2023/09/27/case-study-kodaks-downfall-a-lesson-in-failed-digital-transformation-and-missed-opportunities/.

**The Bottom Line:** The company's failure to adapt to digital technology, despite being an early innovator, serves as a powerful reminder of the dangers of clinging to outdated business models.

## The Downfall Of A Video Rental Giant

In the late 20th century, Blockbuster was synonymous with home entertainment. Incorporated in 1982, the company quickly grew to dominate the video rental industry, with over 9,000 stores worldwide where customers could rent movies and video games, generating revenue through rental fees and late charges.[37]

By the mid-1990s, it had become the leading video rental chain in the United States, acquiring competitors and opening new stores at a rapid pace. The company was so influential that it could dictate terms to movie studios, often securing exclusive rights to rent popular titles. At its peak, Blockbuster was valued at around $3 billion and was considered an unstoppable force in the home entertainment industry.[38]

The first signs of trouble emerged when Netflix was founded in 1997. Initially, Netflix operated as a DVD-by-mail service, which posed a minor threat to Blockbuster's

36. Krause, "Kodak's Downfall," The CDO Times.
37. U.S. Securities and Exchange Commission, "Form 10-K: Data and Reports," SEC.gov, February 16, 2005, https://www.sec.gov/Archives/edgar/data/1085734/000119312505063510/d10k.htm.
38. Andy Ash, "How Blockbuster went from dominating the video business to bankruptcy," *Business Insider*, August 12, 2020, https://www.businessinsider.com/the-rise-and-fall-of-blockbuster-video-streaming-2020-1.

brick-and-mortar model. However, Netflix's introduction of a subscription-based model in 1999, which allowed customers to rent an unlimited number of DVDs for a flat monthly fee, began to erode Blockbuster's market share. Netflix's model also eliminated late fees, a significant source of revenue for Blockbuster, making it an attractive alternative for customers.[39]

Despite these emerging challenges, Blockbuster largely dismissed Netflix as a niche player. In fact, in 2000, Netflix co-founder Reed Hastings approached Blockbuster with an offer to sell the company for $50 million, a deal that Blockbuster's executives famously declined. This decision is often cited as one of the most significant missed opportunities in business history.[40]

As broadband internet became more widespread in the early 2000s, the way people consumed media began to change dramatically. Netflix, always forward-thinking, started to invest in streaming technology, allowing subscribers to watch movies and TV shows directly over the internet. By 2007, Netflix had launched its streaming service, marking the beginning of a new era in home entertainment.[41]

39. "Blockbuster vs Netflix," V500 Systems, February 11, 2022, https://www.v500.com/blockbuster-vs-netflix/.

40. Steve Mollman, "Blockbuster 'laughed us out of the room,' recalls Netflix cofounder on trying to sell company now worth over $150 billion for $50 million," *Fortune*, April 14, 2023, https://fortune.com/2023/04/14/netflix-cofounder-marc-randolph-recalls-blockbuster-rejecting-chance-to-buy-it/

41. "Netflix, Inc.," Encyclopaedia Britannica, last modified April 15, 2023, https://www.britannica.com/money/Netflix-Inc.

Blockbuster, on the other hand, was slow to respond. While Blockbuster had introduced its own streaming service in 2004, it continued to prioritize its traditional rental business. Blockbuster's lucrative in-store model, which had generated billions in revenue, was not something management was eager to step away from. Unfortunately, that hesitation proved to be a costly mistake as consumer behavior shifted toward the convenience of streaming over a physical rental system.[42]

While Netflix's streaming service was gaining in popularity, Blockbuster was in a deep decline. By the time they focused on their own subscription service and elminated late fees, it was too late.

By 2010, Blockbuster was struggling under the weight of $900 million in debt and filed for bankruptcy.[43] The company's store count plummeted, and by January 2014, the last of the company-owned Blockbuster stores had closed.[44]

**The Bottom Line:** Today, Netflix is a global entertainment giant, valued at $302.97 billion, the 33rd most valuable company in the world by market cap,

---

42. Greg Satell, "A Look Back At Why Blockbuster Really Failed And Why It Didn't Have To," *Forbes*, Last updated December 10, 2021, https://www.forbes.com/sites/gregsatell/2014/09/05/a-look-back-at-why-blockbuster-really-failed-and-why-it-didnt-have-to/.
43. Julia Boorstin, "Does Bankrupt Blockbuster Stand a Chance?,"CNBC, September 23, 2010, https://www.cnbc.com/2010/09/23/does-bankrupt-blockbuster-stand-a-chance.html.
44. Lance Whitney, "Blockbuster throws in the towel," CNET, November 6, 2013, https://www.cnet.com/tech/services-and-software/blockbuster-throws-in-the-towel/.

while Blockbuster serves as a case study in missed opportunities and the importance of innovation.[45]

## Do Or Die

The disruptors reshaping the business landscape today aren't just trends, but fundamental shifts that are requiring businesses to rethink how they operate. And when you look at some of the business failure examples that were provided, you may think, that's not relevant for my profession, we don't have technology driving our everyday. But think again.

The disruptor that has my greatest attention right now is Artificial Intelligence (AI) and it should have your attention, too. The AI concept has been around since the mid-20th century, with early developments focusing on creating machines capable of simulating human intelligence. However, it was not until the late 1990s and early 2000s that AI began to integrate into business operations in the form of data analytics, recommendation systems, and automated customer service. Over time, its capabilities have expanded, transforming industries by optimizing processes, enhancing decision-making, and personalizing customer experiences. The rise of generative AI, particularly with tools like ChatGPT, mark a significant leap forward. ChatGPT, launched by OpenAI, is seeing unprecedented adoption, with millions of users embracing the

---

45. "Netflix Market Cap," CompaniesMarketCap, accessed October 16, 2024, https://companiesmarketcap.com/netflix/marketcap/.

technology for a wide range of applications, from content creation to customer support.[46]

This rapid integration of AI is fundamentally changing how businesses operate and is pushing the boundaries of what machines can achieve and forcing a reevaluation of traditional job roles.

For both the marketing and professional services industries over the next three to ten years, AI will continue to revolutionize how we engage with customers by enabling hyper-personalization, real-time customer insights, and predictive analytics. AI-driven tools will continue to allow marketers to create more highly targeted campaigns, optimize content delivery, and automate decision-making processes, significantly increasing efficiency and ROI. According to a report by PwC, AI could contribute up to $15.7 trillion to the global economy by 2030, with marketing and sales being key beneficiaries due to enhanced customer experiences and operational efficiencies.[47]

In the professional services industry, AI is automating many routine tasks, such as document review, data analysis, and financial reporting. This will allow professionals to focus on more complex, value-added

46. "Sizing the Prize: PwC's Global Artificial Intelligence Study: Exploiting the AI Revolution," PwC, accessed October 16, 2024, https://www.pwc.com/gx/en/issues/artificial-intelligence/publications/artificial-intelligence-study.html.
47. Krystal Hu, "ChatGPT Sets Record as Fastest-Growing User Base, Analyst Note," Reuters, February 2, 2023, https://www.reuters.com/technology/chatgpt-sets-record-fastest-growing-user-base-analyst-note-2023-02-01/.

activities like strategic advising and client relationships. A study by McKinsey predicts that up to 23 percent of work activities in the professional services sector could be automated by 2030, leading to increased productivity but also requiring significant upskilling and adaptation from the workforce.[48] The adoption of AI in these industries will drive a transformation in service delivery, creating new opportunities while also posing challenges related to job displacement and ethical considerations.

These stories are a stark reminder of what happens when we get stuck in our own ways. It's pretty clear to see that companies with an Aspiring mindset, who are always on the lookout for what's next, including potential disruptors, will be the ones that not only survive, but will thrive in our ever-changing world. On the other hand, companies that are overly Satisfied and who "check the box," especially when it comes to strategic planning, will find themselves potentially left behind. The changes in technology and societal norms are happening at a lightening speed pace, and those who embrace change will stand out.

*Are you ready?*

---

48. "Generative AI and the Future of Work in America," McKinsey & Company, July 26, 2023, https://www.mckinsey.com/mgi/our-research/generative-ai-and-the-future-of-work-in-america.

# Now What

Here are resources to help you navigate your business's next adaptive challenge. Remember to stay nimble, empower management to pivot when needed, and stay true to your guiding principles and key values.

## Books

- ***The Innovator's Dilemma: The Revolutionary Book that Will Change the Way You Do Business*** by Clayton M. Christensen (Harper Business, 2011). This classic explores why successful companies often fail to innovate and get disrupted by emerging technologies. Christensen introduces the concept of "disruptive innovation" and explains how established companies can avoid being overtaken by more agile competitors.

- ***Only the Paranoid Survive**: **How to Exploit the Crisis Points that Challenge Every Company and Career*** by Andrew S. Grove (Crown Currency, 1999). Written by the former CEO of Intel, this book emphasizes the importance of staying alert to changes in the marketplace and offers strategies for navigating industry shifts and disruptions.

- ***The End of Competitive Advantage: How to Keep Your Strategy Moving as Fast as Your Business*** by Rita Gunther McGrath (Harvard Business Review Press, 2013). Columbia Business School professor and strategic management scholar McGrath examines how long-standing competitive advantages are increasingly rare. Companies need to adapt to constant change and disruption quickly and decisively to thrive.

## Podcast

- ***The Disruptive Voice*** by Christensen Institute: Focused on disruptive innovation, this podcast delves into how companies can anticipate and respond to market disruptions and investigates those that failed to do so.

**Embrace Change**

"Individually we are one drop,
but together we are an ocean."

—*Ryunosuke Satoro*

**5**

VIEW THE ECOSYSTEM
HOLISTICALLY

## ACHIEVE MORE
# TOGETHER

No business entity stands alone, as we are all dependent on each other. In the business world, it's referred to as an ecosystem, or a complex network of interconnected systems. Successful outcomes are achieved when we work in concert—from consumers, to suppliers, distributors, and organizations. We must remain flexible and adaptable, taking the opportunity to learn and innovate together.

W hen was the last time you paused to look not only at your company and competitors but the complete ecosystem that propels your industry? Best-in-class organizations understand that business doesn't happen in a vacuum.

## The What

In today's interconnected business landscape, having a thousand-foot view of your company's complete business ecosystem is paramount for achieving financial success and maintaining a competitive edge. Knowing the industry backward and forward, recognizing the intricate relationships involved, and taking a full inventory of your strengths and weaknesses can help you identify opportunities for growth, innovation, and strategic alliances.

The dream of getting that thousand-foot view finally came true almost fifteen years after forming circle S studio, when I found Drew McLellan, CEO of Agency Management Institute (AMI), through an organic Google search. While I can't recall the exact words of the query, I know it was something like this: How the hell do you run a small marketing and branding agency with more profitability? Bam. Up comes "The Money Matters Workshop for Agency Owners." You've got to love the power of smart thought leadership and a great SEO strategy—otherwise, I would have never found or met Drew McLellan.

The workshop promised attendees interactive sessions and expert-led discussions that would reshape the way we think about the agency's financial management system, walking away with actionable strategies to maximize profits, enhance the agency's value, and ultimately put more money in our pocket. It was being held at Disney's Grand Floridian Resort & Spa in December 2015, and while I didn't know much about AMI or Drew, I thought, what the heck, seems like a no-brainer and if nothing else, it could be a chance to reset and rethink some of our key strategic initiatives.

I don't know about you, but there are a lot of conferences out there, giving you big picture information and sharing case studies that really aren't relevant to what we do, day in and day out. So maybe I came into the whole thing with low expectations, but *oh my gosh*—I was blown away from the moment the workshop started. Every morsel of information was interesting, and every aspect was relevant to our day-to-day operations. This guy truly understood agencies; our only regret is that we hadn't discovered Drew or AMI sooner.

Over two intensive days, agency principals, financial managers, and operations leaders jumped in deep. We focused on what financial metrics were most important, different benchmarks that would guide what a healthy organization our size should look like, how to structure pricing, and proposals to ensure we're not leaving money on the table. Bottom line, we walked away with a clear guide on how to more accurately view our agency's financial health. As it turned out, that workshop was just an appetizer to a whole exquisite menu of offerings.

What I later came to learn is that Drew McLellan had worked in advertising for thirty-plus years and started his own agency, McLellan Marketing Group, in 1995 after a five-year stint at Young & Rubicam.[49] About a decade ago, he was given the opportunity to take over as "head honcho" of Agency Management Institute, that at the time offered a peer group network for like-minded small-to mid-sized agencies. While he didn't start from scratch, what he did was reimagine the mission. He wanted to create a strong community centered around shared learning and mutual trust. He wanted to help agency owners increase their profits, attract better clients and employees, mitigate the risks of being self-employed, and best of all, help agency owners actually enjoy the perks of "owning the joint."

Under Drew's leadership, AMI has grown 900 percent and now serves agencies across the globe with a weekly blog and podcast, "Build a Better Agency," ongoing live and on-demand workshops, leadership coaching, as well as peer groups (both virtual and live).[50] AMI also provides access to a team of trusted advisors that have been "vetted" through a set of high standards that define the organization. It's like a one-stop shop to better understand the best trends in marketing and how to do

---

49. Drew McLellan, email to author, October 15, 2024.
50. Drew McLellan, email to author, October 15, 2024.

everything in terms of running your agency smarter and better.

When I think about the community that he has built, it reminds me of the redwood trees, the tallest and strongest trees on Earth. Not because of deep roots, but because their roots are shallow yet wide, intertwining with those of other redwoods to form a resilient network. By fostering a culture of collaboration and shared learning, Drew has positioned AMI as a leader in the agency industry, demonstrating the power of community in driving both personal and professional growth. He has created an amazing ecosystem that keeps us bettering our best.

So back to looking at your business and your industry from a thousand-foot view, who is helping your firm? What is your competition doing? Who are the various suppliers and organizations working together or separately?

The one thing I have learned is this: There is undeniable power in partnerships. When individuals or organizations come together with a shared vision, the potential for growth, innovation, and success multiplies exponentially. Partnerships allow us to leverage each other's strengths, fill in the gaps where we may lack expertise, and create a synergy that drives greater outcomes than we could ever achieve alone. Whether in business, creative endeavors, or personal development, the collaborative efforts fostered through strong partnerships can lead to groundbreaking ideas, expanded networks, and long-term success.

## So What

When you've done branding and marketing as long as I have, there are few things that are a complete surprise. As we often say, "It's not our first rodeo." But I was struck by an incredible partnership recently that is worth sharing. The way these two organizations came together to create a greater good is incredibly inspiring on many fronts.

Atlantic Bay Mortgage, a regional mortgage lender on the East Coast, was faced, like many firms, with a very competitive landscape. They were seeking innovative ways to differentiate themselves, especially in how they could deliver exceptional experiences for both employees and customers. According to the Chief Lending Officer, Emily Gardner, they wanted something that employees could actively be involved with beyond just giving money to a worthy cause.[51]

After conducting an extensive search and evaluation process, Atlantic Bay Mortgage decided to partner with the Roc Solid Foundation, a growing nonprofit organization dedicated to supporting families of children battling cancer. The decision was driven by several key factors:

**Alignment With Core Values:** The Roc Solid Foundation's mission to "build hope for every child and family fighting pediatric cancer," resonated strongly with Atlantic Bay Mortgage's own values around community engagement and making a tangible difference in people's lives.[52]

**Organizational Fit:** As a regional lender, Atlantic Bay Mortgage was drawn to Roc Solid's focus on local community impact, as well as its plans for geographic expansion that aligned with the mortgage firm's own growth trajectory.

**Engagement Opportunities:** The hands-on volunteer activities offered by Roc Solid, such as packing "ready bags" for families and building custom playsets, provided the type of meaningful, team-building experiences that Atlantic Bay Mortgage was seeking for its employees.

51. "Maximizing Company Volunteer Programs with Emily Gardner [Podcast]," circle S studio, March 31, 2024, https://circlesstudio.com/blog/maximizing-company-volunteer-programs-with-emily-gardner-podcast/.
52. "Our Mission," Roc Solid Foundation, accessed October 16, 2024, https://rocsolidfoundation.org/meet-roc-solid/our-mission/.

**Financial Transparency:** After conducting thorough due diligence on Roc Solid's financials, Atlantic Bay Mortgage was impressed by the nonprofit's commitment to directing the majority of its funding towards its mission-driven programs, rather than administrative overhead.

Their partnership was formalized in 2018 beginning with a clear strategic plan. It was important to each organization to define what success looked like in terms of key performance indicators (KPIs) and how operationally to work in concert at the highest level of communication and feedback.[53] Over the years, they have seen remarkable results, with strong employee participation in Roc Solid volunteer activities. The Atlantic Bay Mortgage culture has seen positive outcomes as well, with an increase in job satisfaction and reduction in employee turnover since the start of the partnership.[54] And the sense of pride in the company's purpose has extended beyond their internal team, as clients often express their appreciation of giving back to families who are affected by pediatric cancer.

In a crowded marketplace, Atlantic Bay Mortgage found a way to STAND OUT. They looked at their ecosystem holistically, which resulted in two unlikely "business partners" coming together to help each other grow. These joint efforts have directly touched the lives of thousands, reflecting the true power of collaboration and making a meaningful difference for all.

---

53. "Maximizing Company Volunteer Program" (Podcast), circle S studio.
54. "Maximizing Company Volunteer Program" (Podcast), circle S studio.

" The partnership with Roc Solid has been transformative for our business, enhancing the employee and customer experience while making a profound impact on families facing unimaginable challenges. It's a true win-win-win."

— *Emily Gardner, Chief Lending Officer, Atlantic Bay Mortgage*

Photo: Roc Solid Foundation.

# Now What

In *The Wide Lens*, Ron Adner introduces the concept of "ecosystem thinking" to understand the interdependencies among business players.[55] Adner suggests that successful innovation requires going beyond a focus on the product or service; it necessitates understanding how various components in the ecosystem work together to deliver value.

## Key Elements Of Visualizing An Ecosystem:

### 1 Value Blueprint

Map out all the stakeholders involved—suppliers, partners, customers, and competitors—and how they interact to create value. The focus is on understanding how your company's "innovation" success depends on your efforts and the contributions and timing of other players in the ecosystem.

### 2 Interdependencies And Risks

Identify the interdependencies and potential risks within the ecosystem. When visualizing your ecosystem, it is crucial to map out the direct interactions and the dependencies that could impact your company. This might include the availability of complementary technologies, regulatory approvals, or the readiness of partners to deliver their components on time.

---

55. Ron Adner, *The Wide Lens: What Successful Innovators See That Others Miss* (Portfolio/Penguin, 2013).

### ③ Co-Innovation And Adoption Chain

Understand how the value of a product or innovation depends on the ability of customers or other players to adopt it. Visualizing these chains helps you see potential bottlenecks or delays that could derail the success of your product/service.

## Example Of A Visual Ecosystem Map

Here's a way to visualize your ecosystem.[56]

- ○ **Central Node:** Core Business (your company, product or service plus core contributors, distribution channels and direct suppliers)
- ○○ **Surrounding Nodes:** Extended Enterprise (including customers, supply chain members, regulators and other stakeholders)
- ······ **Connections:** Interdependencies and interactions that exist between entities
- ➤ **Risks:** Threats or points of failure, like supply chain issues, regulatory changes, or new competitors

---

56. James F. Moore, *The Death of Competition* (New York: HarperCollins, 1997).

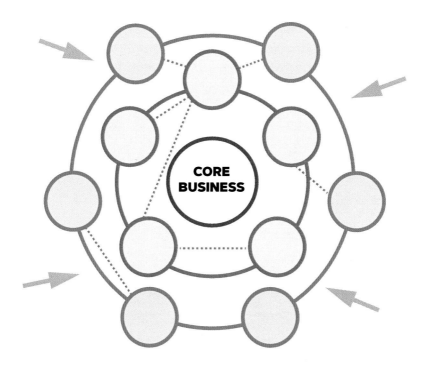

## Books

- **The Wide Lens: What Successful Innovators See That Others Miss** by Ron Adner (Portfolio, 2013). A strategic guide on building successful business ecosystems that includes tools and methodologies for effectively mapping and managing these ecosystems.

- **Platform Revolution: How Networked Markets Are Transforming the Economy—and How to Make Them Work for You** by Geoffrey G. Parker, Marshall W. Van Alstyne, and Sangeet Paul Choudary (W. W. Norton & Company, 2017). For businesses looking to build digital platforms and ecosystems, this book provides strategies for visualizing networks to maximize value for all participants.

## Podcasts

- **HBR IdeaCast** by Harvard Business Review: This podcast brings together leading business voices to discuss various topics, including ecosystem strategies, innovation, and leadership.

- **Masters of Scale** by Reid Hoffman: Hosted by the cofounder of LinkedIn, this podcast explores how entrepreneurs scale their businesses, often highlighting the importance of building and leveraging ecosystems.

NOTES **View The Ecosystem Holistically**

# 6

## TRACK A DATA-RICH DASHBOARD

# UNCOVER
# INSIGHTS
# THAT SPEAK

"It's not what you look at that matters,
it's what you see."

—Henry David Thoreau

Ⓗigh-performing organizations know that building data-rich dashboards is essential for understanding what's working and what areas need improvement, and the operative word here is data-rich. Most companies maintain metrics through a combination of basic tools like spreadsheets, traditional financial reporting, and standard KPIs that track sales, revenue, and customer satisfaction. And many review these metrics regularly—monthly, quarterly, and annually—to gauge their overall business health. The good news is that companies have access to a lot of data, the not-so-good news is that much of this data offers a retrospective view.

That reporting scenario is exactly how we ran the company "back in the day." I craved having a dashboard with real-time data on the "here and now" as well as key information that would help us anticipate future needs and opportunities. I wanted both visual and numerical reporting, I wanted it all, but I couldn't find what I was looking for twenty years ago. There was a lot of software out there but nothing that would visually aggregate everything in front of us. I wanted numbers that would tell a story and wanted that story to be a narrative that was clear to everyone in the company.

# The What

When you combine visuals with numbers, it transforms how we interpret data. Imagine looking at a wall of numbers versus a clean, clear chart. The visuals help you instantly spot trends, outliers, or patterns that might otherwise get lost in the noise. Research even backs this up; well-designed visuals boost comprehension and make decision-making faster. Pairing the two creates a full picture, especially in business dashboards, where seeing both gives you a sharper, faster path to insights that drive smart decisions. It's like turning data into a story that's easier to follow.

In our consulting practice, we often use the following story to encourage companies to enhance their reporting systems.

Think about an airplane's dashboard—it truly is a marvel of engineering, meticulously displaying a vast array of critical metrics in real time. From altitude and airspeed to engine performance and fuel levels, every vital piece of information is presented clearly and intuitively, allowing pilots to monitor the aircraft's status and make precise adjustments as needed.

But what happens if you're looking at the dashboard but not making adjustments as needed? Imagine a plane taking off from Los Angeles, California, on a flight bound for New York City. The pilots have planned the route, accounting for everything from weather patterns to air traffic. However, due to a small, nearly imperceptible error, the plane's course is off by just one degree—a deviation so slight it seems inconsequential at first.

As the plane crosses the country, that one degree deviation begins to compound. Initially, the error might only place the aircraft a few miles off course, but over the span of thousands of miles, this small mistake grows significantly. By the time the plane reaches the East Coast, instead of descending over the iconic skyline of New York City, you are hundreds of miles off target, landing in a completely different location, such as Montreal, Canada. Bottom line, you didn't land where you thought you were going.

While this scenario doesn't happen on a regular basis, it illustrates the critical importance of precision in navigation and decision-making. In the business world, relying on data is crucial, but the real challenge lies in interpreting that data correctly. Just like a plane that's off course by the slightest degree can place you in the wrong state or country, a business that misinterprets its data can find itself far from its intended goals.

## So What

Having a dashboard that tracks key metrics is just the starting point. The real value comes from understanding why these insights matter and how to act on them. Data on financials, customer experience, employee engagement, and operational efficiency are more than numbers—they're opportunities for growth, signals for action, and insights into risk. The question isn't just

Good decision-making requires good data so the ability to collect, analyze and act upon it is essential for sustainable growth and success. In fact, data-driven companies are *23 times* more likely to surpass their competitors in customer acquisition and nearly *seven times* more likely to retain them. Additionally, they are about *19 times* more likely to achieve and maintain profitability.[57]

what the data says, but what you do next to turn it into meaningful outcomes.

When revenue dips or productivity slows, it's not about simply addressing the surface issue, it's about digging deeper. Maybe a drop in customer satisfaction points

57. Alec Bokman, Lars Fiedler, Jesko Perrey, and Andrew Pickersgill, "Five facts: How customer analytics boosts corporate performance," McKinsey & Company, July 1, 2014, https://www.mckinsey.com/capabilities/growth-marketing-and-sales/our-insights/five-facts-how-customer-analytics-boosts-corporate-performance.

to a product problem, or maybe it signals operational inefficiencies. Understanding the "why" ensures companies aren't just reacting but being strategic, leading to smarter resource allocation and innovation driven by real needs, not guesses.

Effective dashboards help translate metrics into action. If employee engagement data shows rising turnover due to a lack of career growth, that's your cue to invest in mentorship or development programs. Similarly, tracking the customer experience can reveal gaps in service, giving you the chance to boost loyalty and increase lifetime value. The difference between companies that thrive and those that fall behind lies in how quickly and effectively they act on these insights.

The best companies aren't waiting for fires to start, they're using dashboards to spot risks before they escalate. This kind of proactive approach ensures they're not just maintaining success but adapting to new challenges, and using data to guide where they are and where they need to go.

## Coca-Cola: Refreshing The World To Make A Difference

Running a successful company for over 100 years is a remarkable achievement that less than half a percent of businesses in the country can even claim. And if you check out the latest list of companies that have reached this milestone, most are familiar names, as you might expect.

At the start of this book, I promised short, concise insights, so here's a quick story about a company that's on that list and they have been "refreshing people everywhere for 138 years." Yes, it's Coca-Cola—one of my favorite brands for its enduring legacy. And honestly, who doesn't love that iconic red logo?

I've always known the basics about the company, that it started in Atlanta, Georgia, with a product derived from two key ingredients: coca leaves and kola nuts. But there's much more to the story.

In 1886, John Stith Pemberton, a curious pharmacist battling a morphine addiction after being wounded in the Civil War, began experimenting with various formulations to ease his suffering. His efforts led to the creation of a caramel-colored syrup, which he marketed as a medicinal tonic at Jacobs' Pharmacy.[58]

---

58. "The Birth of a Refreshing Idea," Coca-Cola Company, accessed October 16, 2024, https://www.coca-colacompany.com/about-us/history/the-birth-of-a-refreshing-idea.

Despite the initial spark of innovation, Pemberton's journey was fraught with challenges. His battle with morphine addiction drained both his finances and his health and the costs associated with his experiments and business ventures only added to his financial woes. Amid mounting debt, he began selling off portions of the rights to his formula, and one of the early buyers was a savvy businessman by the name of Asa Candler, who saw the potential of the formula beyond its medicinal purpose.[59]

Candler gradually bought up more shares, gaining increasing control and after Pemberton's death in 1888, he swiftly acquired the remaining rights, and by 1892 had fully secured ownership and officially incorporated The Coca-Cola Company.[60]

Candler's vision to transform Coca-Cola into a mainstream soft drink involved aggressive marketing and branding, which included distributing coupons for free samples, standardizing the product's production, and emblazoning the logo on various promotional items. This shift in focus from a health tonic to a widely consumed beverage laid the foundation for Coca-Cola's transformation into the brand it is today.

Since Asa Candler's leadership, Coca-Cola has had nine CEOs, each playing a crucial role in the company's evolution.[61] By the mid-20th century, Coca-Cola had

59. The Coca-Cola Company, "Refreshing Idea."
60. "The Asa Candler Era," Coca-Cola Company, accessed October 16, 2024, https://www.coca-colacompany.com/about-us/history/the-asa-candler-era.
61. Tyler Muse, "The History of Coca-Cola's CEOs: Their Accomplishments and Failures," History Oasis, October 1, 2023, https://www.historyoasis.com/post/coca-cola-ceo-history.

established itself as a global powerhouse, but the company recognized that relying solely on traditional methods wouldn't sustain its dominance in an increasingly competitive market. In the early 2000s, Coca-Cola began making significant investments in data analytics and artificial intelligence.[62] These tools allowed the company to gain deeper insights into consumer behavior, optimize its supply chains, and introduce new products that aligned with emerging trends.

Through precise demand forecasting and a commitment to data-driven innovation, Coca-Cola successfully launched products like Coca-Cola Zero Sugar and various flavored waters, catering to the rising demand for healthier options. The company's proactive use of AI further ensured it stayed ahead of market trends. By leveraging historical sales data, weather patterns,

62. "Coca-Cola Leverages Data Analytics to Drive Innovation," Harvard Digital, accessed October 16, 2024, https://d3.harvard.edu/platform-digit/submission/coca-cola-leverages-data-analytics-to-drive-innovation/.

and other external factors, Coca-Cola enhanced its forecasting capabilities, leading to more accurate inventory management. This approach minimized waste and ensured that products were consistently available when and where consumers wanted them.

Today, Coca-Cola's brand is valued at $106.45 billion, with a diverse portfolio available in over 200 countries and territories.[63,64] While its vision, mission, and purpose have evolved, the core focus on refreshment, happiness, and positive impact remains. Coca-Cola's commitment to more than just beverages—creating experiences, inspiring joy, and contributing to the world—has made it a timeless brand.

How would you want your brand story to read 100 years from now?

# Now What

Data literacy is no longer a niche capability. Top-performing companies equip employees at all levels with the skills to interpret and use data effectively for decision-making. The following are some best practices for harnessing the power of data to remain agile and responsive to change.

63. "Coca-Cola's brand value from 2006 to 2024," Statista, July 4, 2024, https://www.statista.com/statistics/326065/coca-cola-brand-value/.
64. "About the Coca-Cola Company," The Coca-Cola Company, accessed September 10, 2024, https://investors.coca-colacompany.com/about.

## Metric Details

### 1 Advanced Business Intelligence (BI)

Advanced BI platforms aggregate data from various sources for a complete, real-time visualization of the business. These platforms help guide quicker, smarter decisions by highlighting trends and patterns that might have gone unnoticed otherwise.

### 2 Focusing On Leading Indicators

While many companies track lagging indicators like sales and profit margins, top performers focus on leading indicators that predict what is coming next—metrics like customer engagement, employee satisfaction, and market trends. These signals offer a glimpse into the future and serve as early warnings for future challenges and opportunities.

### 3 Customizing Dashboards For Different Audiences

Dashboards should provide a personalized road map for each stakeholder to ensure everyone, from top to bottom, has the exact information they need to make informed decisions. Executives get a bird's-eye view, focusing on the key performance indicators that steer the entire organization. At the same time, department heads dive into the detailed metrics that matter most to their specific areas.

### 4 Regularly Reviewing And Updating Metrics

Some companies set their metrics at the start of the year and never look back, but leading organizations take a different approach. They regularly revisit their KPIs, ensuring they stay in tune with shifting business goals and the ever-changing market landscape. This agility allows them to adjust on the fly, ensuring their strategies and priorities always align with the current reality.

You do not know what you do not know. That is why it is important to have the right information at your fingertips. Here are some metrics to consider adding to your dashboard.

## Brand Experience Metrics

1. Brand Awareness (unprompted and prompted)
2. Brand Equity (brand reputation, perceived quality, customer loyalty)
3. Brand Consideration and Purchase Intent Brand Sentiment and Associations
4. Share of Voice
5. Website Traffic and Engagement
6. Social Media Metrics (mentions, reach, engagement)
7. Branded Search Volume

## Employee Experience Metrics

1. Employee Satisfaction
2. Employee Net Promoter Score
3. Employee Engagement
4. Retention and Turnover Rates
5. Internal Referrals
6. Productivity and Performance
7. Diversity and Inclusion
8. Employee Wellness and Burnout

## Client Experience Metrics

1. Net Promoter Score
2. Customer Satisfaction
3. Customer Effort Score
4. Customer Sentiment and Emotional Intensity
5. Customer Retention and Churn Rate
6. Customer Lifetime Value
7. Website/App Metrics (traffic, conversion rates, bounce rates)
8. Support Metrics (response times, first contact resolution)

Here are some additional resources to help you determine your organization's best dashboard.

## Books

- *Information Dashboard Design: The Effective Visual Communication of Data* by Stephen Few (O'Reilly Media, 2006). Data can be both smart and beautiful, according to this classic, on presenting complex data in a way that is aesthetically pleasing and full of actionable insights.

- *The Big Book of Dashboards: Visualizing Your Data Using Real-World Business Scenarios* by Steve Wexler, Jeffrey Shaffer, and Andy Cotgreave (Wiley, 2017). A comprehensive guide to building business dashboards with dozens of examples from real-world companies showcasing different approaches to dashboard design across various industries and business functions.

- *Storytelling with Data: A Data Visualization Guide for Business Professionals* by Cole Nussbaumer Knaflic (Wiley, 2015). While not exclusively about dashboards, this book is invaluable for understanding how to present data visually in a way that tells a clear and compelling story.

## Podcasts

- **Data Stories** by Enrico Bertini and Moritz Stefaner: This podcast explores data visualization, often featuring discussions on dashboard design, data-driven storytelling, and the role of visualization in business intelligence.

- **Data Viz Today** by Alli Torban: This podcast focuses on practical advice for creating effective data visualizations, including dashboards. It is particularly useful for those who want to enhance their skills in presenting data clearly and engagingly.

**Track A Data-Rich Dashboard**

# PART 3:
## Look Within

7

COLLABORATE ON QUALITY

# QA/QC
# IS A TEAM SPORT

> "If it's worth doing, it's worth doing well."
>
> —*Chinese proverb*

There's an underlying rhythm to how most things work together, much like the natural order within a beehive. Just as bees instinctively know their roles and contribute to the hive's success, each person in an organization plays a crucial part in driving the company forward. It's not just about staying busy; it's about ensuring that every action is purposeful and aligned with the larger goals of the business.

## The What

The most successful firms drive every action with a deep commitment to excellence—it's the cornerstone of their business, often driven by strong quality assurance (QA) and quality control (QC) programs. These terms might seem technical or even mundane to some, but the reality is that these programs are the unsung heroes. They ensure that products and services meet the high standards expected by customers, while also safeguarding the brand's reputation. And in an age where information travels at the speed of light, a company's reputation is its most prized asset.

Quality is the primary driver of a sterling reputation. Businesses that consistently deliver high-quality products or services earn the trust and loyalty of their clients. These clients become advocates, spreading positive word of mouth and amplifying the company's brand. It becomes a virtuous cycle, attracting more clients and opening doors to new opportunities.

When there's a lack of quality, the exact opposite can happen. In this chapter, we will delve into the profound impact that a robust QA/QC program can have on your business.

## Winning The Hearts Of Clients

When you have a small company, a robust QA/QC program may not be the first thing you think about, but early on, I realized it was job number one or close to it. The year was 2000, and we had just landed a large national client in the financial industry, and they were going "big" on their advertising spend to spread the word on their new division.

We were developing a lot of ads for industry publications, and like all good ads, we had a CTA—a call to action— which was an 800 number where you could obtain more information. I can still remember sitting at my desk when the president of the division called (and at that time almost all phones were landlines). He wanted to let me know that the number in the ad was incorrect, two numbers inadvertently got switched. I can summarize things simply—he was NOT a happy camper, and all I could muster up was an apology and that I would be in touch by the end of the day with a way to fix the situation. Here's what happened next—we found out that no one owned that phone number, and we were able to set up a way to get the incorrect number redirected to the correct number. We immediately created a new process on how our team would check key information, like a phone number, a mailing address and how we would verify it not once, but twice before files were turned over to the printer or a media publication.

As promised, before the end of the day, I called our client back and told him we had a solution. I shared with him that we had a new QA/QC procedure to ensure the mistake would never happen again, and I also let him know there would be *no charge* for the media costs. I can't remember the exact amount, but it was in the tens of thousands of dollars. A lot of money then and a lot of money today. Bottom line, we "owned it." We had messed up and we had to find a way to fix it. That client is still a client, having moved to several departments during his tenure with that company to the new firm he is with today—and the mistake happened almost twenty-five years ago. He became an advocate because he knew we stood behind a very important part of business: delivering on what we said we were going to do and doing it with quality.

## Fostering A Culture Of Continuous Improvement

One of the most powerful outcomes of a robust QA/ QC program is the cultivation of a culture of continuous improvement. Companies that integrate QA/QC into their daily operations are more likely to embrace innovation and stay competitive in rapidly changing markets. Continuous improvement is about more than just fixing problems—it's about constantly seeking ways to do things better. This mindset leads to better products and services, more efficient processes, and an organization that is always evolving and adapting to new challenges. In the long run, this approach not only drives business success but also keeps the company at the forefront of its industry.

Consumers not only value quality—they expect it, and companies that consistently deliver it see significant benefits. McKinsey reports that businesses prioritizing superior customer experiences through quality products and services can boost customer satisfaction by *20-30 percent*, leading to increased revenue and retention.[65]

65. Victoria Bough, Oliver Ehrlich, Harald Fanderi, and Robert Schiff, "Experience-led growth: A new way to create value," McKinsey & Company, March 23, 2023, https://www.mckinsey.com/capabilities/growth-marketing-and-sales/our-insights/experience-led-growth-a-new-way-to-create-value.

# So What

## Toyota: Quality Assured for Over Eighty Years

We often use the term QA/QC, and if you're anything like me, you probably haven't given much thought to when the whole concept became part of our business vernacular. After doing a little research, I learned that the idea of quality products began in the Middle Ages when standards for membership into the coveted Guild were established for artisans such as cobblers and blacksmiths. During the Industrial Age, we saw quality measures continue to be adopted, especially in the manufacturing sector, to ensure consistency of products. And that's where the Toyota story begins. They not only wrote the playbook, they set the gold standard for QA/QC, making quality synonymous with their brand.

In the late 1920s, a visionary by the name of Sakichi Toyoda, transformed the textile industry with the automatic loom. His revolutionary concept was more than improving efficiency—he wanted to ensure a consistent product that would reduce waste—and his loom would automatically shut down if it detected a problem, like a broken thread. He was proactively seeking ways to prevent defects. Sakichi's approach for constant improvement became the genesis of the Toyota philosophy that we know of today.[66]

The financial success of the automatic loom provided the foundation for his son, Kiichiro Toyoda, to launch the Toyota Motor Corporation in 1937. Kiichiro took his father's principles of quality and continuous improvement and built them into the DNA of the company, creating a culture where innovation and quality have always gone hand in hand.[67]

At the heart of Toyota's operations is the Toyota Production System (TPS), which embeds quality into every step of the manufacturing process. Two core principles define TPS: Jidoka, or "automation with a human touch," which gives every worker the authority to stop production at the first sign of a problem; and Just-in-Time (JIT), which ensures that Toyota produces exactly what's needed, exactly when it's needed. Together, these principles prevent small issues from becoming major problems and keep Toyota's standards consistently high while minimizing waste.[68]

Toyota's commitment to quality has reshaped not only its internal operations but the entire automotive industry. Their vehicles are renowned for durability,

---

66. "Toyota Production System," Toyota, accessed October 16, 2024, https://global.toyota/en/company/vision-and-philosophy/production-system/.
67. "Uncovering the Secrets to Kiichiro Toyoda's Success," AdvisoryCloud, May 30, 2023, https://advisorycloud.com/blog/uncovering-the-secrets-to-kiichiro-toyadas-success.
68. Toyota, "Toyota Production System."

reliability, and longevity, consistently topping rankings for quality and safety. But Toyota's influence extends far beyond the automotive world. The principles behind TPS have inspired management philosophies like Lean Manufacturing and Six Sigma, widely adopted across industries from healthcare to technology.[69]

This attention to detail goes beyond the production line. Toyota's dedication to quality shapes how they interact with customers, build relationships, and adapt to evolving needs. Whether it's pioneering hybrid technology with the Prius or delivering luxury with the Lexus brand, Toyota stays ahead of the curve, ensuring that quality always meets modern demands.

For companies looking to enhance their quality programs, Toyota offers a powerful example. Their long-term success shows that empowering employees, fostering a culture of continuous improvement, and prioritizing real-time problem-solving are essential to sustained excellence. Toyota's story proves that quality isn't just part of success—it's the foundation.

69. Frank Stuart, "Toyota Production System and Lean Management," SST Lift, November 1, 2023, https://www.sstlift.com/blog/toyota-production-system-and-lean-management.

# Now What

Developing a high-quality QA/QC program is crucial for maintaining product and service integrity and customer satisfaction. Here are some of the best resources to help you build a robust program for your company:

## Books

- *The Lean Six Sigma Pocket Toolbook: A Quick Reference Guide to Nearly 100 Tools for Improving Process Quality, Speed, and Complexity* by Michael L. George, John Maxey, David Rowlands, and Mark Price (McGraw-Hill, 2004). A comprehensive guide to the tools and methodologies of Lean Six Sigma—a popular approach for improving quality and efficiency in organizations.

- *Juran's Quality Control Handbook* by J. M. Juran, ed. (McGraw-Hill, 1988). A classic in quality management, this handbook provides deep insights into building and maintaining effective QA/QC programs.

- *Total Quality Management: Key Concepts and Case Studies* by D. R. Kiran (Butterworth-Heinemann, 2016). This book covers total quality management (TQM) principles and includes case studies of companies that have successfully implemented TQM principles.

- ***The Toyota Way: 14 Management Principles from the World's Greatest Manufacturer*** by Jeffrey Liker (McGraw-Hill, 2004). Toyota is renowned for its focus on continuous improvement and high quality standards. This book examines the company's quality management practices.

## Industry Associations And Resources

- **ISO (International Organization for Standardization):** ISO standards, such as ISO 9001 for quality management systems, provide a framework for developing a strong QA/QC program. ISO's resources and certifications are invaluable for companies looking to improve their quality processes.

- **American Society for Quality (ASQ):** ASQ is a global community of quality professionals that offers training, certification, and resources on various aspects of quality management, including QA/QC.

- **Lean Enterprise Institute:** This organization provides resources, training, and publications on lean principles for developing efficient and effective QA/QC programs.

**Collaborate On Quality**

CUT THROUGH THE NOISE

# KEEP IT
## SIMPLE

"If you can't explain it simply, you don't
understand it well enough."

—*Albert Einstein*

D id you ever play the game "telephone" as a child, where one person would whisper something to their neighbor and that message would then get passed down the line? By the time it reached the last person, there was little semblance to what was intended at the start. The same thing often happens in business when our communications get distorted, especially over time, as they get relayed and re-interpreted to others. It's because we're human and we hear and interpret the world differently.

## The What

Businesses can often experience a similar phenomenon with complexity. In the beginning, a process or system is introduced with a clear intent and purpose. But as the company grows, adds new products, and responds to changing markets and regulations, that initial simplicity gets distorted. Layers of procedures are added, new technologies are implemented without fully integrating them, and different departments develop their own ways of doing things. Over time, the original intent behind these systems becomes buried under a tangle of inefficiencies and redundancies.

This chapter underscores the importance of streamlining operations, offering strategies and tools to help companies optimize for efficiency. Simplicity makes a better experience for all—for your employees and for your clients. Think about something as simple as a company handbook. If I start working for you and on day one you give me a fifty-page handbook with thousands of things to know, how much do you think will be retained? The better experience is to guide new employees over a period of time so they understand what is expected and are eager to keep learning more.

So, what's behind all the complication?

It often starts with the way a company is structured. In siloed organizations, each department develops its own processes and systems independently, without considering how they fit into the broader business. This lack of coordination leads to redundancy, conflicting priorities, and miscommunication—all of which contribute to operational inefficiencies and increased complexity.

Legacy systems are another major factor. Many companies rely on outdated processes that were efficient at one point but no longer serve the company's needs. However, replacing them can seem costly or too disruptive, so companies continue to layer new technology on top of old systems. Over time, this creates a fragmented and cumbersome operational environment.

In highly regulated industries, complexity exists on a whole different level. To comply with laws and standards, businesses often implement detailed procedures and systems. While necessary, these systems can lead to an overload of processes that complicate operations, especially when they aren't integrated smoothly into other business functions.

As companies grow, so do the layers of complexity. As new product lines and services get added, especially when keeping up with the competitive landscape, the proper integration into company processes and operations can be overlooked.

And let's not forget our basic human nature that tends to resist change because it disrupts familiar routines and creates uncertainty. Even when we know there's a better way, we avoid adopting new processes or approaches.

Bottom line, when too many initiatives happen at once without a clear strategy, everyone gets stretched thin, teams struggle to align, and complexity creeps in.

In a 2021 *Forbes* article, Kimberly Jansen writes, "Many times we create complexity—the opposite of simplicity. We create it by overcorrecting for issues and making exceptions to the rule. We compensate for underperforming people with absurd workarounds. We also take simple intent and often over-engineer solutions to make people feel better about being included in a process. Much of this is simply unnecessary. The problem is us."[70] Jansen is referring to how individuals overcomplicate things. Now extrapolate that to your organization.

---

70. Kimberly Janson, "The Power Of Simplicity: How To Avoid Over Complicating Things At Work," *Forbes*, May 6, 2021, https://www.forbes.com/councils/forbescoachescouncil/2021/05/06/the-power-of-simplicity-how-to-avoid-over-complicating-things-at-work/.

# So What

In its 2005 Super Bowl ad, office supply retailer Staples made the Easy Button a part of our day-to-day vernacular.[71] Who doesn't want an easy button to take away complexity and provide you with exactly what you want? People have enough on their minds without our company adding to the challenge-induced brain freeze that is modern life. If you can't explain something succinctly or remember it easily, you could be creating a roadblock in your brand, employee, or client experience.

In short, complexity stifles growth, and by focusing on simplification, companies can make decisions faster, innovate more effectively, and better respond to market shifts, all of which contribute to long-term success.

---

71. "Staples Easy Button," Ad Age, February 6, 2005, https://adage.com/videos/staples-easy-button/674.

The consequences of complexity in a business are significant and far-reaching. Complex environments often frustrate employees, leading to demotivation and higher turnover rates. For customers, complexity manifests in lengthy wait times, confusing product offerings, and inadequate support, which ultimately drives them away. On the financial side, complexity contributes to inefficient processes, redundant tasks, and outdated technology, all of which lead to substantial financial losses. Bain & Company reports that simplifying operations can increase profit margins by 25 to 100 percent, highlighting the critical importance of why complexity should be reduced in every organization.[72]

72. Dr. Markus Böttcher and Klaus Neuhaus, "Operational Performance Improvement in Industrial Companies," Bain & Company, June 16, 2015, https:// www.bain.com/insights/operational-performance-improvement-in-industrial-companies/.

# Simplifying For Success

When Steve Jobs returned to Apple in 1997, the company was in a downward spiral.[73] They had a complex and unfocused product line, with multiple versions of the Macintosh computer and an array of other products that were confusing both customers and employees alike. Apple was trying to be everything to everyone, but in doing so, they lost their direction and identity. It was a mess—too many products, too many variations, and none of them truly standing out. Jobs knew he needed to take drastic action to simplify Apple's operations and refocus the company on what it did best.

In a bold move, Jobs slashed Apple's product line by 70 percent.[74] His vision was simple: Instead of spreading the company thin across numerous products, Apple would focus on just a few. He created a clear framework, reducing the product line down to four main categories: consumer desktops, consumer laptops, professional desktops, and professional laptops. This allowed the company to focus on making these four products the best they could be, rather than diluting resources across an unwieldy range of offerings.

---

73. Walter Isaacson, "The Real Leadership Lessons of Steve Jobs," Harvard Business Review, April 2012, https://hbr.org/2012/04/the-real-leadership-lessons-of-steve-jobs.
74. Nick Hobson, "25 Years Ago, Steve Jobs Saved Apple from Collapse: It's a Lesson for Every Tech CEO Today," Inc., April 19, 2023, https://www.inc.com/nick-hobson/25-years-ago-steve-jobs-saved-apple-from-collapse-its-a-lesson-for-every-tech-ceo-today.html.

The results were profound. By narrowing the product focus, Apple could pour its resources and creativity into building high-quality, innovative products like the iMac.[75] They streamlined operations, cutting down on complexity in their supply chain and manufacturing processes, which not only saved money but improved product consistency and customer satisfaction. On top of that, the clarity in their product lineup allowed for much stronger marketing messages. Consumers finally understood what Apple stood for, and they could easily choose the product that best fit their needs.

This strategy didn't just help Apple survive—it set the stage for the company's iconic comeback. With a smaller, more focused product lineup, Apple was able to innovate more effectively, eventually leading to groundbreaking products like the iPod and iPhone.[76] Jobs' commitment to simplifying the product line gave Apple the space to focus on quality, innovation, and user experience, ultimately making it one of the most valuable and admired companies in the world.

This case study is a powerful reminder that sometimes less is more. In an age of increasing complexity, there's real value in narrowing your focus, simplifying your operations, and doing fewer things—but doing them exceptionally well.

---

75. Jason Fell, "How Steve Jobs Saved Apple," Entrepreneur, October 11, 2011, https://www.entrepreneur.com/growing-a-business/how-steve-jobs-saved-apple/220604.
76. "Apple's Innovative Products That Shaped the 21st Century," Bold Business, November 13, 2023, https://www.boldbusiness.com/digital/apple-innovative-products-shaped-21st-century/.

# Now What

Ready to streamline your company's systems and operations? Start with a deliberate and thoughtful approach, and use these steps to root out unnecessary complexity.

### ① Conduct A Comprehensive Audit

Dig into current processes, systems, and procedures across departments to identify areas of complexity, inefficiency, and redundancy.

### ② Engage With Employees

Collaborate with team members across departments to identify the pain points caused by unnecessary complexity.

### ③ Prioritize Areas For Simplification

Focus on simplifying the handful of processes and systems that have the greatest payoff for your firm.

### ④ Phase Out Legacy Systems

Replace outdated technology and reduce approval layers that create bottlenecks.

### ⑤ Audit The Customer Experience

While internal operations are crucial, simplifying processes that improve the customer experience can pay significant dividends, as well.

### 6 Standardize Procedures

Clear, consistent documentation ensures that everyone understands and follows the procedures correctly, reducing the risk of errors and inefficiencies. Make sure all the documentation is easily accessible and regularly updated. Provide training sessions to ensure adoption.

### 7 Monitor And Refine

Simplification is not a one-time event. Be relentless in regularly reviewing processes to ensure complexity doesn't creep back in over time. Avoid the temptation to over-customize systems and workflows so that standardized solutions remain effective across the company.

### 8 Empower Your Team

Foster a culture that values simplicity and efficiency where employees feel empowered to suggest improvements and simplify their workflows.

Here are some great resources for leaders who want to reduce complexity in their operations:

## Books

- **Simplify: How the Best Businesses in the World Succeed** by Richard Koch and Greg Lockwood (Entrepreneur Press, 2016). Learn how successful companies achieve growth by reducing complexity and focusing on simplicity in their products, services, and business models.

- **Essentialism: The Disciplined Pursuit of Less** by Greg McKeown (Crown Currency, 2014). This book makes the case that businesses should focus on eliminating nonessential activities and decisions.

- **The Power of Less: The Fine Art of Limiting Yourself to the Essential...In Business and in Life** by Leo Babauta (Hay House UK, 2009). A practical guide to help you simplify work processes and eliminate unnecessary tasks so you can focus on what truly matters.

## Podcast

- **Lean Blog** by Mark Graban: Interviews with experts on reducing complexity in business processes, improving efficiency, and creating a culture of continuous improvement.

**Cut Through The Noise**

# 9

## COMMIT TO CONTINUOUS LEARNING

# STAY
# CURIOUS

"An investment in knowledge
pays the best interest."

—*Benjamin Franklin*

The final chapter of this book is my all-time favorite trait of the highest-performing companies. And it's pretty basic—they have a mindset and culture of continuous learning and improvement. That's it. They are just always seeking ways to "better their best."

This has certainly been my journey as a business leader and it defines who I want to hang out with. Remember, we're the average of the five people we spend the most time with, so choose wisely. I want that circle of five to be people who constantly ask questions like "Why?", "Why not?", and "What's next?" It's not that they are questioning you—but there's a desire to understand deeper, challenge existing norms, and explore beyond the obvious. This inquisitive approach drives innovation and continuous improvement, as we seek to uncover new possibilities and solutions. Curiosity, in this sense, is the engine behind progress and discovery.

# The What

Staying curious is something I love so much that it has been etched into our company's guiding principles. Our mission is to better our best every day by constantly learning and asking what's next and why. As work continues to evolve, the ability to perpetually learn and problem-solve will be the most sought-after skill in an organization. It's the intersection of high-tech digital dexterity and high-touch soft-skills that can manage as well as coach and mentor. This will keep your company relevant for all generations.

In best-in-class organizations, there is a pervasive culture of improvement. This is not left to a single committee or department. Everyone is looking for ways to make the process a little more efficient, to make the system a little more reliable, to make connections with clients a little more effective and enjoyable. Regardless of the size of your company, improvement means change, and the key is to have a mindset that embraces change.

So how do you build this mindset into the company if it doesn't already exist?

## Top Ways To Institute A Culture Of Continuous Learning:

**1 Lead By Example**

Leaders who remain curious and model lifelong learning will be noticed and emulated by others.

**2 Encourage Open Communication**

When the company culture values sharing knowledge and insights across the organization, especially lessons learned, more questions will be asked, and that's where new ideas for improvement and innovation take root.

**3 Provide Access To Learning Resources**

Incentivize learning and make it easy and accessible to participate. There are many learning styles and the tools that you offer should vary as well, from in-person training, to online courses, to training seminars and conferences.

**4 Promote Experimentation**

We learn the most from things that don't go according to plan and employees should be encouraged to take calculated risks and experiment with new ideas. Learning through experience and even failure should be viewed as a valuable after-action process.

**5 Recognize And Reward Learning**

Acknowledge and celebrate the efforts of those who invest time in learning and development. This can be done through formal recognition, promotions, or incentives tied to educational achievements.

Quickly adapting to change and staying ahead of competitors is essential for business success in our rapidly changing landscape. So how do leaders ensure their companies stay out front? A culture of continuous learning is a critical element. One study found firms that make it a priority are *46 percent* more likely to be industry leaders and *92 percent* more likely to innovate than their competitors. We'd all be wise to learn from these leaders.[77]

# So What

Having a learning-based culture and a team that stays curious, isn't just a nice to have, it's an absolute necessity for spurring growth. Research shows companies that foster a culture of curiosity and encourage ongoing education outperform their competitors in key areas like innovation, employee retention, and profitability. According to a LinkedIn Workplace Learning Report, companies that invest in employee development are

---

77. Neil Bradley, "What Is a Learning Culture? Part 1 of 4," Training Industry, February 22, 2022, https://trainingindustry.com/articles/strategy-alignment-and-planning/what-is-a-learning-culture-part-one-of-four/.

24 percent more likely to hit their long-term financial targets.[78] In an ever-changing business landscape, staying ahead means embracing a mindset of lifelong learning. The ability to adapt, innovate, and grow—fueled by continuous curiosity—can be the deciding factor between thriving and falling behind.

---

**STAND OUT** CASE STUDY

## GORE-TEX

Some of my favorite business success stories are those with humble beginnings, often launched in a home basement. That's how it all started for Wilbert L. (Bill) and Genevieve (Vieve) Gore, when Bill left his job at DuPont in 1958, to pursue a dream of finding ways to tap the potential of a material he found fascinating, PTFE (polymer polytetrafluoroethylene).[79]

W. L. Gore and Associates was known for its flat organizational structure and culture that encouraged continuous experimentation and open collaboration, and it didn't take long for a breakthrough to occur. In 1969, their son, Bob Gore, discovered that he could

---

78. "Empower your workforce and business: Training trends in the TIC business," LinkedIn, April 12, 2024, https://www.linkedin.com/pulse/empower-your-workforce-business-training-trends-tic-bsi-dmdde/.
79. Laila Weigl, "The GORE-TEX Brand: History and Innovations," GORE-TEX, January 13, 2022, https://www.gore-tex.com/en_uk/blog/the-gore-tex-brand-history-and-innovations.

stretch polytetrafluoroethylene under certain conditions, resulting in an incredibly strong, microporous material that was both waterproof and breathable. And just like that, the iconic GORE-TEX fabric was born, a material that we all know today for its high-performance outdoor gear.[80]

Over the years they have continued to innovate using the same outdoor fabric, adapting it for medical devices such as vascular grafts, and even aerospace technology, that sent astronauts into orbit on NASA's Space Shuttle Columbia in 1981, wearing spacesuits made with GORE-TEX.

When you create an environment where employees are empowered to explore, collaborate, and take risks, innovation can be a driver of long-term growth. And GORE-TEX is a prime example of just how powerful that strategy can be with company revenues reaching $3.2 billion in 2023.[81]

Yes, that's what a business success story looks like.

80. "Robert W. Gore," National Inventor's Hall of Fame, accessed October 16, 2024, https://www.invent.org/inductees/robert-w-gore.
81. "W. L. Gore & Associates revenue," Zippia, accessed September 12, 2024, https://www.zippia.com/w-l-gore-and-associates-careers-43900/revenue/

# Now What

Following are some resources for strategies, insights, and tools for leaders who want to encourage a culture of curiosity and continuous improvement.

## Books

- *Mindset: The New Psychology of Success* by Carol S. Dweck (Ballantine Books, 2007). Dweck's research on the "growth mindset" emphasizes the importance of cultivating curiosity and a love for learning. Leaders who adopt a growth mindset are more likely to foster innovation and continual improvement within their teams.

- *The Infinite Game* by Simon Sinek (Portfolio, 2019). An examination of how companies that focus on long-term innovation, learning, and improvement are more successful than those that prioritize short-term gains.

- *The Innovator's DNA: Mastering the Five Skills of Disruptive Innovators* by Jeff Dyer, Hal Gregersen, and Clayton M. Christensen (Harvard Business Review, 2011). A look at the habits of innovative leaders and how curiosity drives creative solutions and organizational growth.

## Podcast

- **The Knowledge Project** by Shane Parrish: A deep dive into the minds of leaders, entrepreneurs, and innovators to explore how curiosity, learning, and decision-making help them learn, adapt, and succeed in business.

## TED Talks

Among the many great TED Talks on the importance of curiosity and continuous learning in business, are:

- **"The Power of Vulnerability"** by Brené Brown, filmed in June 2010, in Houston, Texas. Conversations on the role of vulnerability in fostering creativity and growth.

- **"Do Schools Kill Creativity?"** by Sir Ken Robinson, filmed in February 2006 in Monterey, California. A leader in rethinking the education system discusses the critical role curiosity plays in success.

NOTES **Commit To Continuous Learning**

## Conclusion

What's remarkable about each of the nine traits that we've discussed in this playbook, is how unremarkable they are. They really are basic concepts, yet they are the path to every great company. It's all about consistency, a long-term vision and an even greater stick-to-it-tiveness that's the winner of the day.

I hope the stories and resources provided serve as a starting point for continued growth and self-reflection. Whether you're leading a large organization or a small team, these principles will help you cultivate an environment where every individual can thrive and contribute to the collective momentum.

And speaking of momentum, if you've already taken the nine-trait assessment using the QR code found on page fourteen, make sure you share it with your team. It's an easy way to assess where everyone stands as you design a "cumulative dashboard" for your strategic thinking that will fuel future success.

Regardless of the mindset that shows up for you, STAND OUT firms have a little bit of each one. There are times when it's important to be "Satisfied"—to pause, reflect, and celebrate your accomplishments—don't rush past those moments. Relishing the wins allows you to spread appreciation and recharge yourself, and your team, before tackling what's next.

Everyone needs a "Simplifier" and we learned the importance of making sure complexity doesn't become a burden for your firm. By focusing on streamlining processes and cutting through unnecessary layers, you can bring clarity to your work and enhance productivity across your team.

And those Type A, hard charging, "Aspiring" mindsets, (yep, that's me too) keep thinking about bettering your best. This book is what came out of our Aspiring mindset and what created our podcast—*Better Experiences by Design.* Our vision is to build a community of professionals that are dedicated to sharing their best ideas, learning from each other, and fostering growth through a zealous pursuit of excellence.

So, as you move forward in your own journey, remember that bettering your best is not a one-time goal but an ongoing process. It demands dedication, creativity, and resilience. Set a high bar for yourself and your organization, because, as Walt Disney once said, "If you can dream it, you can do it."

# Acknowledgments

This book is the result of an incredible circle of talent, creativity, and collaboration that has surrounded me throughout this journey. To my long-time business partner, Michelle Davis—your keen eye and attention to detail have been instrumental in shaping our firm's reputation for outstanding design. Thank you for continually pushing us to raise the bar.

To Tami Berry, our strategic thinker extraordinaire — when I floated the idea of conducting third-party research to validate our beliefs on the traits that always show up in high-performing companies, you said "yes, and" with your eternally positive spirit. You are a terrific sounding board, always thinking three steps ahead of me. Like Radar O'Reilly from the famous *MASH* series, you have an uncanny ability to know what I'm thinking even when I haven't fully figured it out myself.

Speaking of third-party research, I'd like to give a special shout out to Susan Baier from Audience Audit. When we first presented our hypothesis to her about what defines a best-in-class company, she responded with a grin stating, "I love it, but my job is to prove you wrong."

When she came back with results, she was delighted to share that we were indeed onto something meaningful. The data showed that the brand, employee, and client experiences do matter—especially to one-third of business leaders. But there's more to it: To resonate with all leaders in the C-suite, your message must go beyond the surface. If it sounds like generic marketing fluff, they will simply tune it out. Thanks to Susan and her team, we were able to better understand the attitudinal mindsets that define a best-in-class community and how to bring these insights to life.

A huge thanks to our exceptional creative team, starting with Michael Couchman, whose cover design captured the essence of this book perfectly. Crystal Cregge (we're so thrilled you chose circle S for your new chapter, after successfully running your own agency) your design expertise, especially in book publishing, gave a lot of depth to the chapters of this book. Thank you, thank you, thank you.

And to Erin Hall Bray, our long-time associate—your dedication, precision, and "can do" attitude are visible in every page of this book. You took a dream and turned it into a work of art. You are best-in-class.

I also know that magic often lies in the details that no one really sees, and for that, a sincere thank you to Sanya Chandler, our Research & Strategy Manager, who ensured every source was meticulously cited. Her thoughtful guidance also led me to new areas of exploration, especially in the *Now What* section, helping to strengthen the depth and accuracy of this book.

Just when you think you've dotted all the I's and crossed all the T's, and perhaps feeling a little "satisified," the outstanding editors of Indie Books International reminded me why it's always wise to bring subject matter experts to the table, especially in areas where you aren't the expert. Henry DeVries, you've pushed me in ways I never thought possible, but most of all, you pushed me to believe in myself—that I could write this book—and I did. For all your support and guidance, I am eternally grateful.

Finally, to the clients we've been honored to serve over the years—thank you for your trust, for giving us the opportunity to help spur growth for your firms, and for teaching me and the circle S team how to continually strive to do everything better.

# Appendix

Chapter 1: Fowlkes, Dick. *Flywheel*. 2018. Painting. Reproduced with permission of Lansing Building Products.

Chapter 2: Bray, Erin. *A Bunch Of Leafy Beets With One That Is Heart-Shaped*. 2024. Generative AI text to image. Adobe Firefly.

Chapter 3: Imaginima. *The Director (Front) - stock photo*. 2007. Photographic rendering. Getty Images, https://www.gettyimages.com/detail/photo/the-director-royalty-free-image/172244662.

Chapter 4: Khasanov, Maxim. *Rock in the form of an eagle's head - stock photo*. 2017. Photograph. Getty Images, https://www.gettyimages.com/detail/photo/rock-in-the-form-of-an-eagles-head-royalty-free-image/813697836.

Chapter 5: Tunart. *Clown Fish hiding in Anemone - stock photo*. 2015. Photograph. Getty Images, https://www.gettyimages.com/detail/photo/clown-fish-hiding-in-anemone-royalty-free-image/476428766.

Chapter 6: Guvendemir. *Passenger airplane taking off at sunset - stock photo*. 2016. Photograph. Getty Images, https://www.gettyimages.com/detail/photo/passenger-airplane-taking-off-at-sunset-royalty-free-image/932651818.

Chapter 7: Dimitrova, Diyana. *Closeup of bees on honeycomb in apiary - stock photo.* 2016. Photograph. Getty Images, https://www.gettyimages.com/detail/photo/closeup-of-bees-on-honeycomb-in-apiary-royalty-free-image/531311994.

Chapter 8: SKT Studio. *Two white paper cups connected with red rope used for classic phone on black stone table board.* Accessed 2024. Photograph. Adobe Stock, https://stock.adobe.com/images/two-white-paper-cup-connect-with-red-rope-used-for-classic-phone-on-black-stone-table-board-for-old-communication-system-concept/177711733.

Chapter 9: LagunaticPhoto. *Funny burrowing owl Athene cunicularia - stock photo.* 2018. Photograph. Getty Images, https://www.gettyimages.com/detail/photo/funny-burrowing-owl-athene-cunicularia-royalty-free-image/964611070.

# About the Author

## Susan P. Quinn

Susan is the founder and CEO of circle S studio, a consultative marketing firm known for propelling growth for clients through exceptional brand, employee, and client experiences. Over the past three decades, she has worked with professionals from Fortune

Photo: Adam Ewing

500 to middle market firms across the country, bringing a keen understanding of how to drive a playing-to-win versus a playing-to-play business strategy that connects sales, branding, and marketing. Her ability to see the big picture and prioritize it into actionable initiatives has created many loyal and long-standing client relationships.

An entrepreneur and lifelong learner at heart, Susan is inspired by bold ideas that move companies and society forward. She explores these themes each month in conversations with other leaders who share a commitment to "bettering their best" on the *Better Experiences by Design* podcast. She is also a certified executive coach and keynote speaker, known for guiding leaders to make meaningful changes that elevate their game in business and in life.

Connect at www.linkedin.com/in/susanquinn01.

Made in the USA
Middletown, DE
14 March 2025